Benjimin Burgher qualified as a barrister in 1995 and is a CIArb accredited mediator. He is now a salaried Employment Judge based in London. He has significant experience of business dispute resolution relating to entitlements, rights, obligations and duties of company directors, partners, LLP members and senior employees. Between 2017 and 2019 he was employed as a Legal Consultant advising the Abu Dhabi Ministry of Justice on the development of labour law and practice and civil litigation processes. He has written numerous articles on employment and discrimination law and regularly provides training to judges and lawyers. He has also presented in the United Nations in Geneva on UAE labour law.

Constructive Dismissal – Practice Pointers and Principles

Constructive Dismissal – Practice Pointers and Principles

Employment Judge Benjimin Burgher
LLB (Hons), PG Dip EC Law, MCIArb

Law Brief Publishing

Published 2020 by Law Brief Publishing, an imprint of Law Brief Publishing Ltd
30 The Parks
Minehead
Somerset
TA24 8BT

www.lawbriefpublishing.com

Paperback: 978-1-913715-38-0

PREFACE

Constructive dismissal occurs where the employer does not dismiss the employee, but the employee resigns and can show that they were entitled to do so by virtue of the employer's conduct.

Recent world events including #Metoo, Black Lives Matter and the COVID-19 pandemic can result in tensions between employers and its employees which in some circumstances can undermine the viability of a continued working relationship. A disagreement with management instructions, including the manner in which the instructions are given, can also lead to an employee resigning. There have been instances of Chinese employees being discriminated at work and verbally abused because of the COVID-19 virus. Sir Philip Rutnam has lodged an employment tribunal claim for constructive unfair dismissal raising bullying and whistleblowing complaints against Home Secretary Priti Patel. Black BBC DJ David Whiteley resigned after the corporation editorial leadership permitted a reporter to use the N-Word in a report. These notable recent matters indicate that constructive dismissal can be frequently misunderstood when referred to in press reports and commentary. In some instances, it is obvious that there has not been proper consideration of what constructive dismissal actually means and in others there is an ignorance of the important necessary elements required to establish it. It is not uncommon to encounter lawyers who also overlook the important necessary elements for constructive dismissal claims.

The aim of this book is to address some of the common mistakes made and misconceptions held by legal professionals when advancing or responding to constructive dismissal complaints. Both the overlaps and important differences between constructive dismissal and constructive unfair dismissal are addressed by reference to relevant precedent illustrating the important principles.

It is hoped that legal professionals will benefit from the eclectic selection of relevant cases and key quotes alongside the important principles summarised in this book in order to be fully prepared to advance or defend constructive dismissal claims in courts and tribunals.

The law stated in this book is believed to be correct at 24 August 2020.

Benjimin Burgher
August 2020

ACKNOWLEDGEMENTS

My partner, Alix for her unending patience and support.

My children, Louis, Alice, Mia and Joseph, and grandson Reuben, for being.

Judge Guy Prichard, colleague and friend, for inspiration.

Margherita Barbagallo and Ploy Wood for their assiduous research.

TABLE OF CASES

Agoreyo v London Borough of Lambeth [2017] EWHC 2019 (QB)

Ahir v BA [2017] EWCA Civ 1392

Argos Ltd v Ms K Kuldo UKEAT/0225/19/BA UKEAT/0439/12/GE

Assamoi v Spirit Pub company (Services) Ltd UKEAT/0050/11/LA

Berkeley Square Holdings -v- Lancer Property Assets Management Ltd [2020] EWHC 1015 (Ch)

Blackburn v Aldi Stores Ltd 0185/12

Brodie v Nicola Ward (First Steps Nursery) UKEAT/0526/07/LA

Brown & Anor v Neon Management Services Ltd & Anor (Rev 1) [2018] EWHC 2137 (QB)

Buckland v Bournemouth University Higher Education [2010] EWCA Civ 121

Chindove v William Morrisons Supermarket Plc UKEAT/0201/13/BA

Cockram v Air Products PLC UKEAT/0038/14/LA Western Excavating (EEC) LTD v Sharp [1978] IRLR 27

Doherty v British Midland Airways Ltd [2006] IRLR 90, EAT

Five Elms Medical Practice v Hayes and another UK/EAT 0345/12/KN

Gebremariam v Ethiopian Airlines Enterprise (t/a Ethiopian Airlines) [2014] UKEAT/0439/12/GE

Gunton v Richmond-upon-Thames London Borough Council [1981] Ch 448

Hogg v Dover College [1990] ICR 39

Holland v Glendale Industries Ltd [1998] ICR 493, EAT

Kaur v Leeds Teaching Hospitals NHS Trust [2018] EWCA Civ 978

Leeds Dental Team Ltd v Rose [2014] IRLR 8, EAT

London Borough of Waltham Forest v Omilaju [2005] IRLR 35

Malik and another (appellants) v Bank of credit and commerce international SA [1997] IRLR 462

Mbuisa v Cygnet Healthcare Ltd [2019] UKEAT/0119/18/B A 8

Mruke v Khan [2018] EWCA Civ 280

Mostyn v S & P Casuals Ltd [2018] UKEAT/0158/17/JOJ

Norwest Holst Group Administration Ltd v Harrison [1985] ICR 66

Pedersen v London Borough of Camden [1981] ICR 674

RDF Media Group PLC and another v Clements [2007] EWHC 2892

Rigby v Ferodo Ltd [1988] ICR 29

Roberts v Governing body of Whitecross School UKEAT/0070/12/ZT

Sandu v Jan De Ruk Transport Ltd [2007] IRLR 519, CA

Singh v Reading Borough Council and another [2013] EWCA Civ 909 CA

Societe Generale v Geys [2012] UKSC 63

Square Global Ltd v Leonard [2020] EWHC 1008 (QB)

Tapere v South London and Maudsley NHS Trust UKEAT/0410/08

Tullet Prebon PLC and others v BGC Brokers LP [2011] IRLR 420, CA

Weathersfield Ltd (T/a Van & Truck Rentals) v Sargeant [1999] IRLR 94

W E Cox Toner (International) Ltd v Crook [1981] IRLR 443

Williams v The Governing Body of Alderman Davies Church in Wales Primary School UKEAT/0108/19/LA

Wright v North Ayrshire Council UKEATS/0017/13

TABLE OF KEY TERMS

CONTENTS

CHAPTER ONE

DEFINITION

Constructive dismissal occurs where the employer does not dismiss the employee, but the employee resigns and can show that they were entitled to do so by virtue of the employer's conduct.

Constructive Dismissal – Common law

The usual starting point for considering a constructive dismissal claim is the Court of Appeal case of *Western Excavating (EEC) LTD v Sharp*[1]. Lord Denning MR set out the principles in paragraphs 15 and 21:

> *If the employer* ***is guilty of conduct which is a significant breach*** *going to the root of the* ***contract of employment;*** *or which shows that the employer no longer intends to be bound by one or more of the essential terms of the contract; then the employee is entitled to treat himself as discharged from any further performance. If he does so, then he terminates the contract by reason of the employer's conduct. He is constructively dismissed.*
>
> ***The employee is entitled in those circumstances to leave at the instant without giving any notice at all or, alternatively, he may give notice and say he is leaving at the end of the notice.*** *But the conduct must in either case be sufficiently serious to entitle him to leave at once.*
>
> *Moreover, he must make up his mind soon after the conduct of which he complains: for, if he continues for any length of time without leaving, he will lose his right to treat himself as discharged. He will be regarded as having elected to affirm the contract.*

---

[1] [1978] IRLR 27

In this case, Mr Sharp was employed by the China Clay Company for 20 months. One of the terms of his contract was that he worked overtime in return for time off in lieu. In February 1976 he asked for 3 hours off from work to play a card game for a team. The foreman refused his request, but he took the time off anyway. The following day the foreman dismissed Mr Sharp with 2 weeks' notice for failing to carry out a reasonable order. Mr Sharp appealed to a panel and they changed the decision to a suspension of 5 working days without pay. Mr Sharp could not meet his expenses over the 5-day period and asked his employers for an advance on his accrued holiday pay, to which they refused. He then asked for a loan and was also refused the amount requested. Mr Sharp resigned in order to get his holiday pay immediately. He made a Tribunal claim for constructive unfair dismissal. This succeeded and he was awarded £658.

Western Excavating's appeal to the EAT was dismissed. On further appeal to the Court of Appeal, it was held that the question to be answered was whether this was in fact constructive dismissal in the context of the wording used in section 95(1) (c) Employment Rights Act 1996, e.g. 'entitled' and 'without notice'.

If the employer is guilty of conduct which is a significant breach going to the root of the contract of employment, or which shows that the employer no longer intends to be bound by one or more of the essential terms of the contract; then the employee is entitled to treat himself as discharged from any further performance. The employer must act reasonably in his treatment of his employees. If he conducts himself or his affairs so unreasonably that the employee cannot fairly be expected to put up with it any longer, the employee is justified in leaving. The test is however one of contract, not one of reasonableness.

If an employee terminates the contract by reason of the employer's conduct, then he is constructively dismissed. The employee is entitled in these circumstances to leave instantly without giving any notice at all, or alternatively he may give notice and say he is leaving at the end of the notice.

The conduct must in either case be sufficiently serious to entitle him to leave at once and he must make up his mind soon after the conduct of which he complains happens. If he continues for any length of time without leaving, he will lose his right to treat himself as discharged.

It was held that the correct test was the contract test because of the legal wording, and they found that the employer did not breach the contract. There would have to be conduct which could bring a contract of employment to an end, which did not exist in this case. Mr Sharp had been guilty of misconduct at work. The Court of Appeal held that the Tribunal decision was a perverse decision based on *whimsy and sentimentality* and therefore the appeal was allowed.

In summary, the necessary elements to be established for constructive dismissal are:

1 Repudiatory breach of the employer;

2 An election by the employee to accept the breach and treat the contract as at an end; and

3 The employee must not delay too long in accepting the breach, as it is always open to an innocent party to waive the breach and treat the contract as continuing.

<u>Constructive dismissal – Statutory definition</u>

Section 95 (1)(c) Employment Rights Act 1996 states:

> *(1) For the purposes of this Part an employee is dismissed by his employer if (and subject to subsection (2) ….. only if-*

> *(c) the employee terminates the contract under which he is employed (with or without notice) in circumstances in which he is entitled to terminate it without notice by reason of the employer's conduct.*

Fundamental breach: terms going to the root of the contract

Fundamental terms of the contract that an employer may breach include cuts in pay or working hours or breaches of the implied terms of trust and confidence or the duty to provide a safe working environment.

It should be relatively straightforward for the employee to prove that the employer has breached a fundamental term of their contract when it relates to cuts in pay or hours. It is more difficult to prove constructive dismissal claims based on breaches of trust and confidence and employees must take care before deciding to resign and claim constructive dismissal on this basis. The courts have found the following breaches of contract to be sufficiently serious to entitle the employee to resign and claim constructive dismissal:

- Reduction in pay or hours.
- Changes in employment duties or employment status.
- Changes in location where there is no mobility clause in the contract.
- Bullying behaviour
- Changes in job responsibilities.
- Not providing work that the employee is employed to do.
- Change in status.

- Excessive workload.
- Failure to address a grievance.
- Unlawful discrimination and victimisation.
- Inept handling of disciplinary matters.
- Intolerable working environment.
- Non-compliance with relevant statutory provisions.
- Breach of the implied term of trust and confidence.
- Arbitrary, capricious, inequitable behaviour.
- Singling out employee and treating them adversely to others.

CHAPTER TWO

THE RELEVANT CONTRACT

Under both common law and statutory constructive dismissal, it is necessary to focus on the terms of the contract and the relevant breach.

Defining the relevant terms

In *Pedersen v London Borough of Camden*[1], the question as to what are the relevant terms of the contract of employment is one of law, however questions as to whether the employer was in breach of contract and, if so, whether the breach was repudiatory (a fundamental breach) are essentially mixed questions of law and fact.

Continued contract following fundamental breach

Constructive dismissal entitles the employee to bring the contract to an end. However, this does not always equate to the termination of the employment relationship. Whilst it is difficult to envisage circumstances where there can be a viable continued employment relationship in circumstances where there is breach of the implied term of trust and confidence, such difficulties do not necessarily arise when there is a breach of express terms and a decision by the employee to work under protest. In such cases the employment relationship will come to an end only when the employee elects to accept the repudiatory breach of contract, following the *Supreme Court in Société Générale (London Branch) v Geys*[2].

---

[1] [1981] ICR 674

[2] [2012] UKSC 63

The House of Lords case of *Rigby v Ferodo Ltd*[3], considered an actual and intended continuation of the relationship of employer and employee without interruption where there was a repudiation of contract. The repudiation was a reduction in pay. The employee worked on under protest but claimed breach of contract. At page 35B of the case Lord Oliver saw "*no reason in law or logic why, leaving aside...the extreme cases of outright dismissal or walk-out, a contract of employment should be on any different footing from any other contract as regards the principle that 'an unaccepted repudiation is a thing writ in water...*" The argument that the employee impliedly accepted the repudiation by working on under protest was rejected. As there was no termination, the deductions from wages were ongoing.

Separate contract following termination

Whilst not a constructive dismissal case, *Hogg v Dover College*[4], EAT is often cited as a basis for claiming constructive dismissal when a change in the term(s) of the contract takes place. In 1986, the applicant, who was a full-time teacher and department head became ill and following a period of absence returned to teaching part-time. On 31 July 1987, the headmaster wrote to him expressing the view that his ill health made it impossible for him to continue as department head and offering him fewer teaching periods at a considerably reduced salary. The applicant replied claiming that the letter amounted to a dismissal but that pending his claim of unfair dismissal he would continue to work at the college on the terms offered. On his complaint of unfair dismissal an industrial tribunal found that the letter did not amount to a summary dismissal but rather that it was a statement that his employment would continue on different terms and that by continuing to work at the college, he had accepted the employers' repudiation of his contract of employment. Consequently, he had not been constructively dismissed.

---

[3] [1988] ICR 29

[4] [1990] ICR 39

In *Hogg* at page 42E, Garland J found that the employee "*was being told that his former contract was from that moment gone*". To the employer's argument that there was no dismissal, only a variation, Garland J stated at page 42F:

> *"It seems to us, both as a matter of law and common sense, that he was being told that his former contract was from that moment gone. There was no question of any continued performance of it. It is suggested, on behalf of the employers, that there was a variation, but again, it seems to us quite elementary, that you can vary by consent terms of a contract, but you simply cannot hold a pistol to somebody's head and say: "henceforth you are to be employed on wholly different terms which are in fact less than 50 per cent, of your previous contract." We come unhesitatingly to the conclusion that there was a dismissal on 31 July."*

The EAT held that Mr Hogg had been actually dismissed by the imposition of a demotion, but that Garland J stated at page 42G "*even if we were wrong about that, we would take the view that there was a constructive dismissal*". Mr Hogg had from the outset claimed that his contract had been terminated and agreed to work on new terms, while reserving his rights.

Fundamental breach cannot be cured

In *Buckland v Bournemouth University Higher Education Corporation*[5], the Court of Appeal concluded that a repudiation cannot be cured by the guilty party. At paragraphs 40 and 43, Sedley LJ stated that once a fundamental breach has occurred, "*all the cards are in the hand of the wronged party*" and "*the option of acceptance or affirmation [is] in the innocent party's hands*". At paragraph 52 Jacobs LJ said "[*The employee] should have a clear choice: affirm or go. Of course the wrongdoer can try to*

[5] [2010] EWCA Civ 121

make amends – to persuade the wronged party to affirm the contract. But the option ought to be entirely at the wronged party's choice."

Buckland was approved by the Supreme Court in *Société Générale (London Branch) v Geys*[6]. At paragraph 18, Lord Hope stated that "*the party who is in the wrong should not be permitted to benefit from his own wrong*". At paragraph 97, Lord Wilson stated the law seeks "*to protect the innocent party, as far as practicable, from the consequences of the other's breach*".

Therefore, following the Court of Appeal case in *Buckland*, and endorsement by the Supreme Court *Geys*, requiring the employee to elect to end the contract following a repudiatory breach, it is very difficult to see how *Hogg* can now be considered to be relevant authority for constructive dismissal cases.

6 [2012] UKSC 63

CHAPTER THREE

EXPRESS TERMS

Courts and Tribunals are required to assess whether the employer has acted in repudiatory breach of contract or, for statutory purposes, whether the employer's conduct entitles the employee to terminate the contract without notice. There is little practical distinction between the two. However, invariably there is a requirement to undertake a careful assessment of what constitutes a repudiatory breach of contract. The more straightforward cases involve assessing whether there has been a breach of express terms of the contract.

Obviously, contracts can vary; they can be written or oral. If oral, there is a requirement to determine what the express terms actually are. Whilst oral employment contracts continue to exist, whether due to ignorance of the law, tax avoidance, exploitation of workers or a combination of the above, it is likely that over time they will become less prevalent. From 6 April 2020, section 1 of Employment Rights Act 1996 was extended to require the provision of a statement of initial particulars at the beginning of the employment, which will invariably record the express terms of the contract that a court or tribunal will be required to construe. Section 1 Employment Rights Act 1996 (Updated to include workers from 6 April 2020) is set out at Appendix A.

It should take little effort to persuade a court or tribunal that a breach of an express term of contract amounts to a breach of a fundamental term of the contract entitling the employee to resign without notice.

Changes to the express terms by the employer without consent of the employee are likely to form a basis for constructive dismissal. The key point is to check the contract and assess whether the employer has failed to comply with the contractual terms.

Pay cut

In *Mostyn v S & P Casuals Ltd*[1], the EAT considered whether enforcing a pay cut constituted a breach of the implied term of trust and confidence. The case was considered under a breach of the implied term as it was a proposed pay cut, i.e. an anticipatory breach of contract, rather than an actual pay cut.

The Claimant was employed as a sales executive. From 2012 – 2016 his sales figures fell. In 2016 the Respondent asked him to accept a pay cut (from £45,000 to £25,000). The Claimant wrote to the Respondent saying it was trying to remove him from the business and that their actions were so severe he considered his contract as having been breached. The Respondent treated the letter as a grievance, which it rejected, indicating the changes to his contract would be actioned. The Claimant resigned with immediate effect.

The Claimant brought a claim for constructive unfair dismissal, alleging that the imposition of a pay cut was both a breach of an express contractual term and of the implied term of trust and confidence.

The Employment Tribunal ("ET") considered the following test for determining whether an action amounts to a breach of an implied term:

i Is the Respondent's action likely to destroy or seriously damage the relationship of trust and confidence (objective test); and

ii Was the action carried out without reasonable or proper cause?

The ET found the second limb of the test was not met. The Respondent had reasonable cause (dwindling sales and the Claimant was not improving his sales performance). The ET found no breach of

[1] [2018] UKEAT/0158/17/JOJ

either an implied or fundamental term of the contract and dismissed the claim for constructive dismissal. It further found that even if he had been dismissed, it would have been fair because it related to his capability.

The Claimant appealed to the Employment Appeal Tribunal ("EAT") and argued that the ET erred in asking whether the employer had reasonable and proper cause for imposing the salary change because there had been a repudiatory breach of an express term in relation to salary.

Laing J allowed the appeal. She held at paragraph 3 that *...a reduction in pay is almost always, if not always, repudiatory unless it is consented to...*

At paragraph 55 of the judgment she stated that an employer cannot have a reasonable and probable cause for breaching the implied term where the breach consisted of the unilateral imposition of a significant pay cut on an employee.

Specific express variation clauses

Some contracts have express mobility clauses which give the employer a right to unilaterally make variations to the contract, such as the right to assign duties, change hours of work and/or suspend without pay. Such express clauses must be carefully assessed, and in any event, considered in the context of the implied term of trust and confidence when considering the employer's communication of the relevant changes to the employee and whether it properly addressed any concerns raised by the employee regarding the impact of such changes.

CHAPTER FOUR

BREACH OF IMPLIED TERM OF TRUST AND CONFIDENCE

The implied obligation extends to any conduct by the employer likely to destroy or seriously damage the relationship of trust and confidence between employer and employee.

When considering the scope of the implied term of trust and confidence parties cannot go wrong by referring to the House of Lords case of *Malik and another v Bank of Credit and Commerce International SA*[1]. At paragraph 60, Lord Steyn stated:

> *The implied obligation extends to any conduct by the employer likely to destroy or seriously damage the relationship of trust and confidence between employer and employee. It may well be, as the Court of Appeal observes, that the decided cases involved instances of conduct which might be described 'as conduct involving rather more direct treatment of employees': [1966] ICR 406, 412. So be it. But Morritt LJ held that the obligation (p.441B-C): '... may be broken not only by an act directed at a particular employee but also by conduct which, when viewed objectively, is likely seriously to damage the relationship of employer and employee.'*
>
> *That is the correct approach. The motives of the employer cannot be determinative, or even relevant, in judging the employees' claims for damages for breach of the implied obligation. If conduct objectively considered is likely to cause serious damage to the relationship between employer and employee a breach of the implied obligation may arise.*

---

[1] [1997] IRLR 462

In *Leeds Dental Team Ltd v Rose*[2], Judge Burke QC stated at paragraph 25:

> *"The test does not require a Tribunal to make a factual finding as to what the actual intention of the employer was; the employer's subjective intention is irrelevant. If the employer acts in such a way, considered objectively, that his conduct is likely to destroy or seriously damage the relationship of trust and confidence, then he is taken to have the objective intention spoken of..."*

The House of Lords in *Malik* decided that the behaviour of the employer need not necessarily be focused on the employee and the implied obligation extends to any conduct by the employer likely to destroy or damage the relationship of trust and confidence. The House of Lords held that:

1. Damages for loss of reputation caused by breach of contract may be awarded provided that a relevant breach of contract can be established, and the requirements of causation, remoteness and mitigation can be satisfied.

2. It was not accepted that in order to constitute a breach of the implied term, the trust destroying conduct must be directed at the employee. The implied obligation extends to any conduct by the employer likely to destroy or seriously damage the relationship of trust and confidence between the employer and employee. If conduct objectively considered is likely to cause damage to the relationship between employer and employee, a breach of the implied obligation may arise.

---

[2] [2014] IRLR 8 (EAT)

CHAPTER FIVE

DISCIPLINARY, SUSPENSION AND GRIEVANCE PROCEDURES

Buckland

The Court of Appeal in *Buckland v Bournemouth University Higher Education*[1] is a good starting point for considering the importance of adhering to proper processes. The claimant, Professor Buckland, worked for Bournemouth University. As part of his role he marked papers annually for the university. In the 2006 marks he concluded that there were 16 resists of which 14 papers failed. The second marker endorsed those marks. At a meeting attended by the claimant and the board of examiners and chaired by Dr Astin, the results were checked and verified. The programme leader shortly afterwards took it upon himself to re-mark the papers and the marks were not far away from what the claimant had suggested but some students could be moved up by combining the marks from other papers. The claimant protested about the re-marking and the university set up an enquiry chaired by Professor Vinney. The claimant found that Professor Vinney was not independent enough to chair the enquiry, so he declined to attend. The report from the enquiry vindicated the claimant, stating that his marks should have been final and making constructive proposals for improvements in the future. The claimant was unhappy with the report because in it Dr Astin questioned his integrity and Dr Vinney supported Dr Astin's comments on his integrity. A Professor Darville set out to mollify the claimant by telling him that the university should have never put itself into such a position. The claimant did not accept this, and he resigned by letter on 22 February 2007 and brought proceedings for unfair constructive dismissal.

---

[1] [2010] EWCA Civ 121

The following issues were raised:

1. Is the occurrence of a fundamental breach of a contract of employment, at least on the employer's part, to be gauged by a conventional contract test or by a 'range of reasonable responses' test?

2. Does the law permit a party which has committed a repudiatory breach of a contract of employment to preclude acceptance by curing the breach?

3. If it does, was the tribunal's decision that the university had failed to cure its breach of the claimant's contract of employment (i) legally sound and (ii) factually tenable.

4. Did the university advance a triable case that, if there had been a constructive dismissal, had been fair? If it did, the tribunal overlooked it and, if necessary, the respondent seeks a remission.

It was held that the circumstances that can bring about a constructive dismissal are created in the common law. The common law holds that they must be circumstances amounting to a fundamental or repudiatory breach of contract by the employer. It was accepted that reasonableness is one of the tools the employment tribunal can use for factual evidence but it cannot be a legal requirement. It was held that there was no need to assess the employer's behaviour by reference to a 'range of reasonable responses' test when deciding whether there has been a breach.

The Court of Appeal then went on to consider the issue described above. In paragraph 22 the Court of Appeal referred to the "proliferation of recent authority and dicta" on the issue, "not all of it consistent". At paragraphs 22 and 23, Sedley LJ endorsed the reasoning of the EAT on this issue. It was as follows:

> *"(1) In determining whether or not the employer is in fundamental breach of the implied term of trust and confidence the unvarnished Mahmud [Malik] test should be applied.*
>
> *(2) If applying the Sharp principles, acceptance of that breach entitled the employee to leave, he has been constructively dismissed.*
>
> *(3) It is open to the employer to show that such dismissal was for a potentially fair reason.*
>
> *(4) If he does so, it will then be for the Employment Tribunal to decide whether dismissal for that reason, both substantively and procedurally ... fell within the range of reasonable responses and was fair."*

In the Court of Appeal case of *Kaur v Leeds Teaching Hospitals NHS Trust*[2], Underhill LJ made some general observations about the extent to which disciplinary and grievance processes can found constructive dismissal claims. At paragraph 63 Underhill LJ noted that an employee exercising a right of appeal is unlikely to amount to an unequivocal affirmation of contract and at paragraph 75 he observed that an employer properly following its disciplinary process and/or the outcome of such a process, cannot amount to, or contribute to, a repudiatory breach of contract.

Grievance procedure

The EAT case of *Assamoi v Spirit Pub Company (Services) Ltd*[3] looked at whether a near breach can be averted. The Claimant worked as a head chef. He had rather a turbulent period of employment with his employer. The ET made a finding that the Claimant's manager had acted in a way likely to damage the relationship of trust and confidence.

---

[2] [2018] EWCA Civ 978

[3] [2012] UKEAT/0050/11/LA

However, in the investigation senior management vindicated the Claimant's position.

The ET found that this prevented the acts of the immediate manager constituting a breach of the implied term. The main ground of the appeal was that this was a misdirection in the light of *Bournemouth University Higher Education Corporation v Buckland*[4] (CA). This was rejected on the basis that the facts of the case were very different. Judge Pugsley held that:

> *"We consider that, properly construed, the decision amounts to findings by the tribunal that, although Mr Cooper had behaved badly towards the Claimant, his behaviour was not so serious as to justify the Claimant leaving and there was a finding that the fair minded way in which the investigatory meeting proceeded was such that it prevented the matter escalating into a state of affairs that would have justified the Claimant leaving and claiming he was constructively dismissed."*

It was held that there is a distinction between preventing matters escalating into a breach of the implied term of mutual trust and confidence and trying to cure a breach which has already taken place.

The EAT distinguished *Buckland* in this case because the manager's conduct on its own was not enough to seriously damage trust and confidence and their subsequent actions prevented the matter from escalation. Trust and confidence is usually destroyed by a series of events, not one small event. At paragraph 36 Judge Pugsley stated:

> *We do not consider that we should move into the area of metaphysical abstraction. There is a fundamental distinction, which it is perhaps more easy to recognise than to define, between there being a fundamental breach of contract that an apology by an employer*

---

[4] [2010] EWCA Civ 121

cannot cure and there being action by an employer that can prevent a breach of contract taking place. The members of this Tribunal with industrial experience point out that the whole object of a grievance procedure and a disciplinary procedure is that an employee has the opportunity to articulate his concerns about the behaviour of management and to defend himself against allegations that in some way he is unfit to remain in the employment of the employer.

If, for example, in a large industrial undertaking an employee called John Smith were to be given notice of a disciplinary hearing concerning a sexual assault perpetrated by him on a female employee, and it later transpired that due to an administrative mix-up the letter should have been sent to another employee of the same name, would the recipient of the first letter, sent in error, be entitled to say there had been a breach of an implied term, albeit that as soon as he had taken up the matter there was a profuse apology and an acceptance that the recipient of the letter was wholly innocent of any such inappropriate behaviour? It might be that the most cursory enquiries by the employer would have revealed that the recipient of the letter did not work on the same site or in the same section as the female employee concerned and may indeed have never met her. In those circumstances, we venture to suggest that an Employment Tribunal would consider that the employer's prompt apology for the mistake and the removal of the apprehension that the recipient of any such letter would undoubtedly have, might well be said to have prevented such a breach. However, if the employer had not acted to check the protests of the innocent employee and allowed the matter to drag on before finally accepting the mistake must have been made by them, then different considerations might apply.

In the EAT case of *Blackburn v Aldi Stores Ltd*[5] it was part of the Claimant's case of constructive dismissal, based upon the implied term of trust and confidence, that the Respondent effectively denied any proper appeal against its decision upon a grievance which he had presented. The ET did not determine this issue regarding it as irrelevant to the Claimant's case concerning the implied term of trust and confidence. This was an error of law.

The Claimant also sought to amend the claim to plead that the grievance procedure in question had contractual effect. The amendment was refused. This was an error of law. HHJ Richardson made the following observations:

> *25 – In our judgment failure to adhere to a grievance procedure is capable of amounting to or contributing to such a breach. Whether in any particular case it does so is a matter for the Tribunal to assess. Breaches of grievance procedures come in all shapes and sizes. On the one hand, it is not uncommon for grievance procedures to lay down quite short timetables. The fact that such a timetable is not met will not necessarily contribute to, still less amount to, a breach of the term of trust and confidence. On the other hand, there may be a wholesale failure to respond to a grievance. It is not difficult to see that such a breach may amount to or contribute to a breach of the implied term of trust and confidence.*

Disciplinary procedure

The EAT case *Five Elms Medical Practice v Hayes and another*[6] considered what constitutes a breach and what employers must ensure when discussing potential disciplinary matters with employees.

---

[5] [2013] UKEAT/0185/12
[6] [2013] UKEAT 0345/12/KN

Mrs Hayes and Mrs Tilley worked for Five Elms Medical Practice. A complaint was raised about them by another employee to the soon to be staff lead. The complaint suggested that staff members had left the practice due to Mrs Hayes and Mrs Tilley's management style and there was also a complaint of bullying.

A meeting was called for both Mrs Hayes and Mrs Tilley and they were not given notice of their meetings. They were both shown written complaints and told to respond there and then. They both raised informal grievances with their employer and neither grievance was dealt with before they resigned. Both claimants resigned and brought claims for constructive unfair dismissal and their claims were upheld. HHJ Clark dismissed the respondent's appeal on the basis that the ET applied the correct law to the facts and considered matters objective per *Malik* and that there was no perversity in the decision.

Suspension

In the case of *Agoreyo v London Borough of Lambeth*[7] Foskett J looked at the issue of suspension.

The Claimant was a teacher with 15 years' experience who entered into a fixed term contract to work in the Respondent's primary school. She was suspended after 5 weeks following 3 incidents involving children with challenging behaviour (she had physically removed them from the classroom). The Claimant alleged that she was entitled to use force in the circumstances and that she had not used more than reasonable force within theEducation and Inspections Act 2006, section 93(1).

The Respondent said the suspension was a precautionary "neutral action" and that she would have an opportunity to attend an investigation meeting where she could provide her account of the events. The

[7] [2017] EWHC 2019 (QB)

Claimant submitted a handwritten resignation letter on the same date as her suspension letter, which she claimed she had written before she received notice of her suspension. She brought a claim against the Respondent for damages for breach of contract. The County Court dismissed her claim and she appealed.

The appeal was allowed based on the following:

1 The suspension from employment was not a neutral act and should not be a routine response to the need for an investigation.

2 Employers should avoid using suspension as a default position without consideration of the alternatives and should carry out further investigation into the allegation before deciding whether to suspend.

CHAPTER SIX

MISCELLANEOUS BREACHES

<u>Breach of statutory provisions</u>

Employees frequently rely upon breach of statutory rights, such as failure to pay minimum wage, breach of Equality Act 2010 provisions, or detrimental treatment following raising discrimination complaints or protected disclosures for whistleblowing complaints. However not all breaches of statutory provisions amount to a fundamental breach of contract entitling a worker to resign and claim constructive dismissal.

In *Doherty v British Midland Airways Ltd*[1], HHJ McMullen QC stated at paragraph 29:

> *"That is just a brief snapshot as to why MsRayner's proposition is wholly misconceived in our judgment. It cannot be right that .... the range of rights set out in [the Butterworth Employment Law Handbook], which takes pride of place on our bench, constitutes a contractual rulebook, actionable at the suit of an employee for every single breach that there is. The sole basis upon which her proposition was advanced was a passage in a book written by MrSelwyn, in which he says that certain aspects of the statute may be the source of contractual terms. That of course is true of Equal Pay Act 1970, the National Minimum Wage Act 1998, the Working Time Regulations 1998, and other statutes which directly affect the contractual relationship. But in our judgment it does not provide a justification for the implication of a contractual term covering precisely the same territory as the statute. We reject this contention."*

---

[1] [2006] IRLR 90 (EAT)

In the case of *Mruke v Khan*[2], the Court of Appeal considered the issue of whether there can be a repudiatory breach of contract on account of less favourable treatment where the employee is ignorant of his or her rights.

The Claimant was a 54-year-old illiterate Tanzanian national who had been employed by the Respondent as a domestic worker. She previously worked at a hospital in Tanzania run by the Respondent. She came to the UK in 2006 and worked in the Respondent's home until 2010 when she left the employment.

The ET allowed her claims for unlawful deduction of wages, arising from the Respondent's failure to pay her the national minimum wage rate, holiday pay or give proper rest breaks. The ET dismissed her claims for race discrimination and constructive unfair dismissal. The ET found that she had not been treated less favourably than a hypothetical comparator. Whilst failure to pay minimum wage was a repudiatory breach, the Claimant had not known she was entitled to minimum wage and had not resigned in response to that breach. The EAT dismissed her appeal.

The Court of Appeal allowed the Claimant's appeal in part on the basis that the ET erred in its approach regarding her claim for constructive unfair dismissal (which was based on the employer's failure to pay national minimum wage). The fact that the Claimant had been unaware of her entitlement to minimum wage did not prevent the failure amounting to a repudiatory breach of contract. However, she had not been directly discriminated against on racial grounds. Her socio-economic circumstance, not nationality or national origins, was the reason for the less favourable treatment.

In *Ahir v BA*[3], the Court of Appeal considered the threshold required for striking out a claim when it has no reasonable prospect of success.

---

[2] [2018] EWCA Civ 280

[3] [2017] EWCA Civ 1392

The Claimant was employed as a member of the ground staff with airside security clearance. The Respondent's HR department received an anonymous letter stating the Claimant had lied on his CV regarding the reason for him leaving his former employment and that he had been dismissed for misconduct. Following disciplinary hearings, the Respondent dismissed the Claimant for misconduct arising from the dishonesty involved in his false CV.

The Claimant brought claims against the Respondent for victimisation, discrimination, unfair dismissal and wrongful dismissal. He admitted he lied on his CV but contended that the Respondent had already been aware of the circumstances of his departure from his previous employer, and that it had concocted the anonymous letter as part of a plan to get rid of him.

The ET struck out the dismissal claims (under ET Regs Sch.1 para 37). It concluded that the allegations were founded on baseless and unlikely assertions and had no reasonable prospect of success. The remainder of the claims proceeded to a full hearing (but were ultimately dismissed).

The Claimant appealed the strike out and argued that the ET's decision had not reflected the high threshold required for striking out claims as having no prospect of success. The Claimant contended that only in exceptional circumstances should the draconian measure of striking out be appropriate. The EAT dismissed the appeal. It found that the Claimant's case was fanciful and that the ET had been entitled to strike out the claims.

The Claimant appealed the EAT decision to the Court of Appeal, which was also dismissed. The Court of Appeal found that whilst unfair dismissal claims based on discrimination and victimisation were fact sensitive and should usually proceed to a hearing, especially where the facts are in dispute, the ET should not be deterred from striking out claims (under ET Regs Sch.1 para 37), even where there were disputed facts, provided that they were satisfied that they had no reasonable prospect of success.

Breach of contract – Health and safety standards

In *Mbuisa v Cygnet Healthcare Ltd*[4], HHJ Eady QC (as she then was) considered whether a breach of contract arose in relation to health and safety standards.

The Claimant's employment ended after less than a year following sick leave for 3 months. He had insufficient length of service for an unfair dismissal claim so he brought a claim for breach of contract, unauthorised deductions from wages and holiday pay, race and disability discrimination, and constructive unfair dismissal on the grounds of public interest disclosures and for health and safety reasons.

The Claimant alleged breaches of the implied obligation to maintain trust and confidence based on various acts of disability and race discrimination, and the Respondent's failure to act on his complaints about breach of safety procedures. He also claimed that he had resigned because of the Respondent's breach of the implied duty to take reasonable care for his health and safety, and that his constructive dismissal was automatically unfair because the sole, or principal, reason for his dismissal was that he took one of the health and safety related actions identified by section 100 ERA.

The ET struck out the claim for constructive unfair dismissal for a health and safety reason. It concluded that the Claimant was not suggesting that the matters that had caused him to resign (assaults and being required to carry out lifting work when he was not fit to do so) had occurred by reason of any actions he had taken for section 100 ERA purposes.

[4] [2019] UKEAT/0119/18

HHJ Eady QC held that the ET erred in striking out this claim as it had assumed a case for the Claimant that did not fully engage with what he was trying to say. While the immediate reason(s) why he left his employment (the assaults, threatened assault and requirement to do lifting work) might not have occurred directly because of anything he had said or done relevant to section 100, the Claimant was saying that the Respondent had allowed circumstances to exist such that these things could happened because of his section 100 concerns. The question for the ET was whether there was no reasonable prospect of the Claimant being able to show that his raising of matters falling under section 100 was the reason or principal reason for why the Respondent allowed circumstances to arise such that he could be assaulted, threatened with assault or required to do lifting work.

The ET's decision to strike out could not stand and was set aside. It was held that the appropriate course of action to take in this case was to record how the case was in fact being put, ensure that the original pleading was formally amended and make any appropriate deposit order if it was considered that the case had little reasonable prospect of success. HHJ Eady QC allowed the Claimant's appeal. The claim was remitted to the ET under section 100 for consideration with the other claims. This decision was on the basis that:

1 The claim for constructive unfair dismissal for a health and safety reason should not have been struck out since, although it was badly pleaded, there was a case with a prospect of success.

2 The ET failed to understand the Claimant's case on automatic constructive unfair dismissal under section 100.

CHAPTER SEVEN

ANTICIPATORY BREACH

There will be no constructive dismissal if the employee resigns after the employer has withdrawn his threat to break the contract. This was confirmed by the Court of Appeal in *Harrison v Norwest Holst Group Administration Ltd*[1]. The employer has the opportunity at any time before communication of the acceptance of the repudiation to alter his stance and withdraw the threat of breach of contract. The same cannot be said for actual breaches which cannot be cured.

Buckland v Bournemouth University Higher Education[2] considered whether it was possible for the employer to 'cure' a repudiatory breach of contract by attempting to make amends or undo what has been done. If the employee has affirmed the contract then it can be taken that the breach was cured. But if the employee has not affirmed then the employee has a right to choose whether to treat the breach as final. It is noteworthy that in the EAT in *Buckland* a distinction was found between an anticipatory breach which has not yet occurred (and would never occur if cured) and a completed breach which once occurred can never be undone.

Sedley LJ stated at paragraphs 43 and 44:

> ... ***why, if on those general principles an anticipatory breach can be cured up to the moment of acceptance, a completed breach cannot be.*** *The answer has to be that the anticipatory or threatened breach has by definition not yet occurred and, if withdrawn, never will. A completed breach, even if it can be compensated for, cannot be undone. The only hint of a doctrine of cure of completed breaches that counsel have been able to show us is in the judgment in W E*

---

[1] [1985] IRLR 240, [1985] ICR 668

[2] [2010] EWCA Civ 121

Cox Toner v Crook (above), where the EAT said, citing Farnworth Finance Facilities Ltd v Attryde [1970] 1 WLR 1053:

".... However, if the innocent party further performs the contract to a limited extent but at the same time makes it clear that he is reserving his rights to accept the repudiation or is only continuing so as to allow the guilty party to remedy the breach, such further performance does not prejudice his right subsequently to accept the repudiation"

But this formulation explicitly leaves the option of acceptance or affirmation in the innocent party's hands.

44 Albeit with some reluctance, I accept that if we were to introduce into employment law the doctrine that a fundamental breach, if curable and if cured, takes away the innocent party's option of acceptance, it could only be on grounds that were capable of extension to other contracts, and for reasons I have given I do not consider that we would be justified in doing this. That does not mean, however, that tribunals of fact cannot take a reasonably robust approach to affirmation: a wronged party, particularly if it fails to make its position entirely clear at the outset, cannot ordinarily expect to continue with the contract for very long without losing the option of termination, at least where the other party has offered to make suitable amends. The present case, for reasons explained by Jacob LJ, may be seen as the kind of exception which proves the rule.

<u>Settled intention to breach</u>

Where there is a settled intention to breach the contract that has not yet occurred then there could still be a breach of contract.

In the case of *Roberts v Governing Body of White Cross School*[3], the EAT considered whether a school's communicated intention to pay half rather than full pay during a period of sickness absence amounted to a fundamental breach of contract.

Following allegations made against him, the Claimant went on sick leave in November 2009. In March 2010 the Deputy Head wrote to the Claimant notifying him that he would be placed on half pay from 28 May 2010. On the same day the Claimant wrote to the Deputy Head asking for confirmation that he would be paid in accordance with the Burgundy Book, the collective agreement that applied to his contract.

An email was subsequently sent to the Claimant suggesting that the 'industrial injury' cover only related to physical injury and not the Claimant's stress at work. On 26 May 2010 the Claimant resigned. The ET concluded that the Respondent was in breach of contract by not paying 100% of pay while the Claimant was off sick. The basis of this decision amounted to a fundamental breach of contract.

Slade J held that a settled communicated intention to pay half rather than full pay was a fundamental breach of contract. The conclusion of the ET that the established breach was not fundamental because of an honest, though mistaken, view of the meaning of the relevant contractual term was erroneously relied upon the judgment of an Employment Judge. On the findings of fact by the ET, including that the Respondent had a settled intent to pay 50% of full pay, no other conclusion could be reached other than the Respondent was in anticipatory breach of contract. The EAT distinguished between adopting a view of a contractual obligation and acting on that view. The case was remitted to a differently constituted ET for rehearing on whether there was a clear and settled intention not to honour the contract.

---

[3] UKEAT/0070/12/ZT

In *Mostyn v S & P Casuals Ltd*[4], Laing J considered whether enforcing a pay cut constituted a breach of the implied term of trust and confidence. The case was considered under a breach of the implied term as it was a proposed pay cut (anticipatory breach of contract) rather than an actual pay cut. The Claimant had relied on a threat to unilaterally impose a substantial cut in his basic pay (before commission) as a breach of the implied term of trust and confidence. The ET held that the Claimant resigned because of the breach and that the breach was a breach of the implied term, but that the Respondent had reasonable and probable cause for imposing the pay cut. Laing J held that, given that the breach relied on was a significant breach of an important express term (as well as a pleaded breach of the implied term) the ET had erred in law in asking itself whether the employer had reasonable and probable cause for repudiating the contract of employment. It was held that the ET's conditional decision that any dismissal was unfair could not stand. The case was remitted to a different ET for it to consider whether or not the Claimant was unfairly dismissed.

[4] [2018] UKEAT/0158/17/JOJ

CHAPTER EIGHT

THE FINAL/LAST STRAW

The final straw doctrine states that an employee can resign in response to a series of breaches of contract or a course of conduct by their employer which taken cumulatively amounts to a breach of the implied term of trust and confidence.

The last incident in the chain can often be unsubstantial but can be sufficient to render the whole series of incidents as a breach of the implied term. The test is whether, viewed objectively, the course of conduct showed that the employer over time had demonstrated an intention to no longer be bound by the contract of employment.

The oft-quoted Court of Appeal case of *London Borough of Waltham Forest v Omilaju*[1] considered what acts can count as the last straw and whether there can be a constructive dismissal claim where the employers' final act which prompted the resignation is found by the tribunal to be reasonable conduct.

Mr Omilaju was employed by the Council and he issued 5 sets of ET proceedings against them. The ET dismissed all his claims. The Council refused to pay him his full salary for July and August when he had been absent with leave in order to attend the tribunal hearing. The Council policy was for employees to take annual leave or unpaid leave in such circumstances. Mr Omaliaju resigned from his role stating that the refusal to pay him was the last straw in a series of unfavourable treatments over a period of years which had destroyed his trust and confidence. He then issued a claim for constructive unfair dismissal. This claim was dismissed. The ET found that the Council's refusal to pay the Claimant was reasonable and justifiable and acting fully within

---

[1] [2005] IRLR 35, See Dyson LJ at paragraphs 15 – 22

his contract and therefore it could not be viewed as the last straw. However, the EAT allowed Mr Omaliaju's appeal against that decision and also granted the employer's leave to appeal.

On appeal to the Court of Appeal, the Council argued that although the final straw does not need to be a breach of contract, it must at least be conduct which is blameworthy or unreasonable. Mr Omilaju argued that it cannot be a requirement that the final straw should amount to blameworthy or unreasonable conduct since that would in itself amount to a breach of the implied term of trust and confidence and therefore also a breach.

In his decision, Dyson LJ considered the final straw doctrine (at paragraph 14):

> ***14 The law***
>
> *The following basic propositions of law can be derived from the authorities:*
>
> *1. The test for constructive dismissal is whether the employer's actions or conduct amounted to a repudiatory breach of the contract of employment: Western Excavating (ECC) Ltd v Sharp [1978] IRLR 27.*
>
> *2. It is an implied term of any contract of employment that the employer shall not without reasonable and proper cause conduct itself in a manner calculated or likely to destroy or seriously damage the relationship of confidence and trust between employer and employee: see, for example, Malik v Bank of Credit and Commerce International SA [1997] IRLR 462, 464 (Lord Nicholls) and 468 (Lord Steyn). I shall refer to this as 'the implied term of trust and confidence'.*

3. Any breach of the implied term of trust and confidence will amount to a repudiation of the contract see, for example, per Browne-Wilkinson J in Woods v WM Car Services (Peterborough) Ltd [1981] IRLR 347, 350. The very essence of the breach of the implied term is that it is 'calculated or likely to destroy or seriously damage the relationship' (emphasis added).

4. The test of whether there has been a breach of the implied term of trust and confidence is objective. As Lord Nicholls said in Malik at p.464, the conduct relied on as constituting the breach must 'impinge on the relationship in the sense that, looked at objectively, it is likely to destroy or seriously damage the degree of trust and confidence the employee is reasonably entitled to have in his employer' (emphasis added).

5. A relatively minor act may be sufficient to entitle the employee to resign and leave his employment if it is the last straw in a series of incidents. It is well put at para. [480] in Harvey on Industrial Relations and Employment Law: '[480] Many of the constructive dismissal cases which arise from the undermining of trust and confidence will involve the employee leaving in response to a course of conduct carried on over a period of time. The particular incident which causes the employee to leave may in itself be insufficient to justify his taking that action, but when viewed against a background of such incidents it may be considered sufficient by the courts to warrant their treating the resignation as a constructive dismissal. It may be the 'last straw' which causes the employee to terminate a deteriorating relationship.'

When considering what amounts to a final straw, Dyson LJ continued at paragraphs 19 – 22:

19 The question specifically raised by this appeal is: what is the necessary quality of a final straw if it is to be successfully relied on by the employee as a repudiation of the contract? When Glidewell

LJ said that it need not itself be a breach of contract, he must have had in mind, amongst others, the kind of case mentioned in Woods at p.351 where Browne-Wilkinson J referred to the employer who, stopping short of a breach of contract, 'squeezes out' an employee by making the employee's life so uncomfortable that he resigns. ***A final straw, not itself a breach of contract, may result in a breach of the implied term of trust and confidence. The quality that the final straw must have is that it should be an act in a series whose cumulative effect is to amount to a breach of the implied term. I do not use the phrase 'an act in a series' in a precise or technical sense. The act does not have to be of the same character as the earlier acts. Its essential quality is that, when taken in conjunction with the earlier acts on which the employee relies, it amounts to a breach of the implied term of trust and confidence. It must contribute something to that breach, although what it adds may be relatively insignificant.***

20 I see no need to characterise the final straw as 'unreasonable' or 'blameworthy' conduct. It may be true that an act which is the last in a series of acts which, taken together, amounts to a breach of the implied term of trust and confidence will usually be unreasonable and, perhaps, even blameworthy. But, viewed in isolation, the final straw may not always be unreasonable, still less blameworthy. Nor do I see any reason why it should be. The only question is whether the final straw is the last in a series of acts or incidents which cumulatively amount to a repudiation of the contract by the employer. The last straw must contribute, however slightly, to the breach of the implied term of trust and confidence. Some unreasonable behaviour may be so unrelated to the obligation of trust and confidence that it lacks the essential quality to which I have referred.

21 ***If the final straw is not capable of contributing to a series of earlier acts which cumulatively amount to a breach of the implied term of trust and confidence, there is no need to examine the earlier history to see whether the alleged final straw***

does in fact have that effect. *Suppose that an employer has committed a series of acts which amount to a breach of the implied term of trust and confidence, but the employee does not resign his employment. Instead, he soldiers on and affirms the contract. He cannot subsequently rely on these acts to justify a constructive dismissal unless he can point to a later act which enables him to do so. If the later act on which he seeks to rely is entirely innocuous, it is not necessary to examine the earlier conduct in order to determine that the later act does not permit the employee to invoke the final straw principle.*

22 Moreover, an entirely innocuous act on the part of the employer cannot be a final straw, even if the employee genuinely, but mistakenly, interprets the act as hurtful and destructive of his trust and confidence in his employer. The test of whether the employee's trust and confidence has been undermined is objective (see the fourth proposition in paragraph 14 above).

The Court of Appeal held that the EAT had erred and restored the ET judgment. It was concluded that:

1 In order to result in a breach of the implied term of trust and confidence, a final straw, not itself a breach of the contract, must be an act in a series of earlier acts which cumulatively amount to a breach of the implied term.

2 The act does not have to be of the same character as the earlier acts if, when taken in conjunction with the earlier acts on which the employee relied, it amounts to a breach of the implied term of trust and confidence.

3 If the employer has committed a series of acts which breach the implied term but the employee does not resign and affirms the conduct he cannot subsequently rely on those acts to justify a constructive dismissal if the final straw is

entirely innocuous and not capable of contributing to the earlier acts.

4 The final straw viewed in isolation need not be unreasonable or blameworthy conduct.

5 The mere fact that the alleged final straw is reasonable conduct does not necessarily mean that it is not capable of being a final straw although it will be an unusual case where conduct that has been viewed objectively to be reasonable and justifiable satisfies the final straw test.

6 The test of whether the employee's trust and confidence has been undermined is objective.

In *Kaur v Leeds Teaching Hospitals NHS Trust*[2], the Court of Appeal elaborated on the doctrine of the last straw by finding that the concept of affirmation of contract is not strictly relevant in last straw cases. What is required for last straw resignation is that a series of incidents, whether or not previously affirmed, amounts to a fundamental breach of contract.

In this case, there was an altercation between an employee and another staff member resulting in the employer taking disciplinary action. The disciplinary panel found the employee guilty of inappropriate behaviour and she was given a final written warning. Her disciplinary appeal was dismissed, and she resigned the next day. She brought a claim for constructive unfair dismissal, relying on a series of events amounting to a breach of the implied term of trust and confidence (i.e. alleged unjustified complaints about her performance, the altercation and the conduct of the disciplinary and appeal proceedings). The employer's application to strike out the claim succeeded on the basis that the ET

---

[2] [2018] EWCA Civ 978

found no reasonable prospect of success. The EAT dismissed the employee's appeal.

The Court of Appeal found that further contributory acts effectively 'revive' an employee's right to rely upon the whole series of acts, notwithstanding earlier affirmation(s). If the employee does not delay in their resignation from the last of these incidents, their claim will be well-founded.

Underhill LJ, at paragraph 55, noted that there are 5 questions to consider when determining whether the last straw doctrine applies:

1 What was the most recent act (or omission) on the part of the employer which the employee says caused, or triggered, the resignation?

2 Has the employee done anything to suggest that they have accepted (or affirmed) the contract since that act?

3 If not, was that act (or omission) by itself a repudiatory breach of contract (i.e. of sufficient importance to justify resignation)?

4 If not, was it nevertheless a part of a course of conduct comprising several acts and omissions which, viewed cumulatively, amounted to a repudiatory breach of the employee's contract by showing that all trust and confidence had been destroyed? If it was, there is no need for any separate consideration of a possible previous affirmation.

5 Did the employee resign in response (or partly in response) to that breach?

He concluded that none of those questions is conceptually problematic, though of course answering them in the circumstances of a particular case may not be easy.

At paragraph 63, Underhill LJ noted that an employee exercising a right of appeal is unlikely to amount to an unequivocal affirmation of contract, and at paragraph 75 he observed that an employer properly following its disciplinary process and/or the outcome of such a process, cannot amount to, or contribute to, a repudiatory breach of contract.

Ultimately, the Court of Appeal found that the ET was entitled to conclude the claim had no reasonable prospect of success and so the appeal was dismissed. However, even if a final straw is innocuous, it does not necessarily mean that all previous conduct by an employer is irrelevant.

In the EAT case of *Williams v The Governing Body of Alderman Davies Church in Wales Primary School*[3], the Claimant appealed the ET's findings that he was not unfairly or constructively dismissed and the ET's rejection of his claim of failure to make reasonable adjustments. The EAT allowed the appeal.

The Claimant, who is disabled by reference to a mental impairment, worked as a teacher for the Respondent. He was suspended because of what he was told was a child protection matter and, after more than a year of disciplinary investigation, he resigned. He brought claims in the ET for unfair constructive dismissal and constructive dismissal amounting to disability discrimination, but the ET found that the Claimant had not been dismissed, and so the claims failed. The Claimant appealed, challenging amongst other things the ET's conclusions that he was not constructively dismissed, and hence the rejection of the unfair dismissal claim.

---

[3] UKEAT/0108/19/LA

HHJ Auerbach held that the ET erred in concluding that, because it had found that the conduct of the Respondent which tipped the Claimant into resigning could not contribute to a breach of the implied duty of trust and confidence, his claim that he was constructively dismissed must fail. That would be correct only had it properly found that:

(a) there was no prior conduct by the Respondent amounting to a fundamental breach; or

(b) there was, but it was affirmed. But if, in such a case, there was prior conduct amounting to a breach which was not affirmed, and which also materially contributed to the decision to resign, the claim of constructive dismissal will succeed.

HHJ Auerbach held at paragraph 34:

> *"so long as there has been conduct which amounts to a fundamental breach, [the breach has not been affirmed], and the employee does resign at least partly in response to it, constructive dismissal is made out. That is so, even if other, more recent, conduct has also contributed to the decision to resign."*

On the facts found, had the ET applied the law correctly, it would have found that there was a constructive dismissal. It had found that there was prior conduct which contributed to the decision to resign, and which amounted to a breach of the implied term. It could not have properly found that such conduct had been followed by affirmation. A finding of constructive dismissal was therefore substituted.

CHAPTER NINE

EXCEPTIONS

Without prejudice communications

Subject to establishing that an exception to the without prejudice rule applies, an employee is not able to rely upon without prejudice communications as part of the evidence to found a claim for constructive dismissal. Roth J provided a comprehensive recent summary of the exceptions at paragraphs 43 – 47 in the case of *Berkeley Square Holdings -v- Lancer Property Assets Management Ltd* [1], namely:

1 That a settlement agreement has been reached;

2 That an agreement should be set aside on the ground of misrepresentation, fraud or undue influence;

3 An estoppel argument;

4 Perjury, blackmail or other unambiguous impropriety;

5 To explain delay or apparent acquiescence;

6 That a party has taken reasonable steps to mitigation loss when that party has put the reasonableness of the settlement in issue (the "Muller" expectation);

7 That a settlement agreement should be rectified (an extension to the first exception); and/or

8 To aid the interpretation of a settlement agreement.

[1] [2020] EWHC 1015 (Ch)

In the case of *Brodie v Nicola Ward (First Steps Nursery)*[2] the EAT considered the last straw doctrine and without prejudice letters. The Claimant was employed as a teacher and Deputy Head of the First Steps Nursery School. The Respondent was the new owner of the nursery. The Claimant brought a claim for unfair constructive dismissal stating that she had been wrongfully denied contractual sick pay and that she had resigned when she received a letter from the Respondent's solicitors written to propose a settlement in respect of sick pay. She claimed that the letter was the last straw which led to her resignation.

The Respondent denied repudiating the Claimant's contract of employment and argued that the solicitor's letter which had been sent was protected by privilege. It was marked 'without privilege' and could not be relied upon, and therefore could not found a constructive dismissal claim. The ET agreed that the letter was privileged under the without prejudice rule and was not subject to any of the exceptions to that rule.

On an appeal, no issue arose as to whether the solicitors letter fell within the without prejudice rule because the Appellant agreed that it was so. The issue was whether one of the two exceptions to the without prejudice rule, namely dishonesty and/or unambiguous impropriety, applied to the letter.

The EAT, chaired by HHJ Birtles, concluded that the letter did not fall within any of the exceptions to the without prejudice rule and was therefore privileged. It held that the ET was correct in excluding a solicitor's without prejudice letter in other proceedings which the Appellant claimed was the "last straw" causing her to resign and claim constructive dismissal. As such, Ms Brodie could not disclose her employer's proposal for the termination of her employment to rely on as amounting to the last straw for her claim for constructive unfair dismissal.

---

2 UKEAT/0526/07/LA

Protected conversations

Protected conversations under section 111A of the Employment Rights Act 1996 provide little tangible protection against constructive dismissal claims. Protected conversations have very limited scope and such a conversation could provide the basis for an employee to raise a grievance arising from what may be perceived as unwarranted and previously uncommunicated concerns about performance or behaviour and result in an allegation that the implied term of trust and confidence has been undermined.

Judicial proceedings immunity

Judicial proceedings immunity is the principle that those involved in the judicial process should be immune from civil suit for what they do or say in the course of the litigation. Therefore, the contents of pleadings and witness statements responding to claims should usually be immune.

However, in the Court of Appeal case of *Singh v Reading Borough Council & Or*[3] two principles were addressed, namely the principle that a wrong should not be without a remedy, and the principle that those involved in the judicial process should be immune from civil suit for what they do or say in the course of the litigation.

In September 2009 Ms Singh was appointed Headteacher of Moorlands Primary School. The Governing Body of the school had statutory responsibility for Ms Singh's appointment and for the management of her performance and the implementation of policies regulating the employment relationship, including grievance, capability and disciplinary procedures.

---

[3] [2013] EWCA Civ 909 CA

One of the members of the Senior Leadership Team at the school was Sue Heath, the School Business Manager and Clerk to the Governing Body. Ms Heath worked closely with Ms Singh, and they had a good working relationship. During Ms Singh's first year as Headteacher serious difficulties arose in her relationships with parents, members of staff and governors, including the Chair of the Governing Body. Ms Singh alleged that, right from the start, she was met with hostility and aggression in response to her attempts to take forward the strategic management of the school; that the governors deliberately endorsed a targeted campaign of discrimination, bullying, harassment and victimisation against her as an Asian Headteacher; and that the Council, deliberately and unlawfully endorsed a targeted campaign of discrimination, bullying and harassment and victimisation against her to remove her as head of the primary school. The allegations were denied, and it was contended that there was a serious breakdown in relationships due to Ms Singh's autocratic style of leadership and her poor communication skills.

On 14 June 2010, the Council received a petition signed by approximately 170 parents, expressing a vote of no confidence in Ms Singh. On 16 June 2010 the Council decided to appoint an independent investigator, Ms Barnes-Vachell, to conduct a review of the school. In her interim report, sent by email on 2 July, Ms Barnes-Vachell expressed serious concerns about the school, referring to it as "a school at risk" and describing an air of chaos. She recommended that Ms Singh be removed from her post pending the outcome of the review. In consequence, Ms Singh took a period of voluntary paid leave pending the outcome of the review.

Ms Barnes-Vachell presented her final, draft report to Ms Singh and the Council on 18 July. Ms Singh complained that this report was neither informed nor impartial, and that the integrity of the investigation was undermined by the investigator's failure to act fairly, in circumstances where she was on leave and was unable to refute the findings until the evidence gathered was provided to her.

On 21 July Ms Singh lodged a formal grievance complaining of race discrimination and victimisation, including allegations against the Council relating to the conduct of the investigator's review. On 3 September, an external consultant, Minna Nathoo, was appointed to investigate the grievance. Interviews with thirty people, including Ms Singh and Sue Heath, were tape recorded and transcribed during this investigation, which continued until December 2010.

On 14 September 2010 the Claimant issued her ET1, complaining of race discrimination, harassment and victimisation against her by the Council and the governors. The allegations reflected those already made in her grievance. On 15 October the Council filed a detailed ET3 denying all the allegations.

Subsequently, the ET proceedings progressed. Ms Singh asserted that she telephoned Sue Heath on 22 and 26 November 2011, to ask if she would be a witness for her at the hearing. She received a text message from Mrs Heath on 26 November, which read as follows: "*Dear Sudhana, I have been instructed to have no contact with you and to refer you to Sonal Khimji at rbc, regards Sue*".

On 31 January 2012 witness statements were exchanged in readiness for the forthcoming Tribunal hearing. The statements served by the Council included a witness statement from Sue Heath.

On 17 February 2012 Ms Singh wrote to the Chair of the Governing Body and resigned from her employment with effect from 17 July 2012. She referred to having suffered psychiatric injury, as a result of her treatment by the Council. In addition, she said:

> *"By reference to all the complaints of discrimination I have raised previously I have effectively been dismissed from my post and I have no alternative but to resign.* ***We recently exchanged witness statements for the Tribunal and the statement from Mrs Susan Heath is ridden with blatant lies, and I believe that she has been***

> ***forced to provide such a statement of 'untruths' deliberately and directly to undermine me for the purposes of the tribunal claim. I believe this conduct to be unacceptable and demonstrative of bad faith on the part of my employer and in breach of the duty of trust and confidence and fidelity. When I read Mrs Sue Heath's statement I was shocked and deeply upset and my health very quickly deteriorated. I regard this as the latest in a series of acts whereby I have been discriminated against and victimised for having raised my complaints of discrimination …***
>
> *…I am deeply devastated that the Governing Body that you Chair and Reading Borough Council has failed to exercise its duty of care for me throughout my tenure and which makes my position now untenable due to a very clear breakdown in the trust and confidence between us."*

On 17 February 2012 Ms Singh applied to the ET to amend her ET1 to add claims of constructive discriminatory dismissal, constructive unfair dismissal and to allege that she had suffered psychiatric injury as a result of her treatment. Further, Ms Singh sought to amend her ET1 to allege:

> *"The Claimant further relies on the Respondent's conduct in placing undue pressure on Mrs Sue Heath to produce a witness statement containing false or otherwise inaccurate evidence for the purpose of these proceedings."*

The issue was whether that amendment should be allowed to be made. Both the ET and EAT (on appeal) held that her allegation should not be permitted because judicial proceedings immunity covered all the Council's activities (whether proper or improper) in gathering evidence for the purpose of defending Ms Singh's claim of discrimination.

On appeal to the Court of Appeal it was concluded that the pressure allegedly applied on Ms Heath amounted to a free standing act. The complaint was not about the contents of the statement and it was alleged that the pressure applied on Ms Health was calculated to destroy the mutual term of trust and confidence.

Lewison LJ summarised at paragraph 66 that:

1 The core immunity relates to the giving of evidence and its rationale is to ensure that persons who may be witnesses in other cases in the future will not be deterred from giving evidence by fear of being sued for what they say in court;

2 The core immunity also comprises statements of case and other documents placed before the court;

3 That immunity is extended only to that which is necessary in order to prevent the core immunity from being out-flanked;

4 Whether something is necessary is to be decided by reference to what is practically necessary;

5 Where the gist of the cause of action is not the allegedly false statement itself, but is based on things that would not form part of the evidence in a judicial enquiry, there is no necessity to extend the immunity;

6 In such cases the principle that a wrong should not be without a remedy prevails.

CHAPTER TEN

AFFIRMATION, WAIVER, ELECTION AND DELAY

Affirmation

Lord Denning MR held at paragraph 15 of *Western Excavating v Sharp*[1]:

> *Moreover, he must make up his mind soon after the conduct of which he complains: for, if he continues for any length of time without leaving, he will lose his right to treat himself as discharged. He will be regarded as having elected to affirm the contract.*

The leading case on the doctrine of affirmation is *W E Cox Toner (International) Ltd v Crook*[2], which applies where an employer is in fundamental breach of an employee's contract. Mr Justice Browne-Wilkinson stated:

> *"13. … **Mere delay by itself (unaccompanied by any express or implied affirmation of the contract) does not constitute affirmation of the contract;** but if it is prolonged it may be evidence of an implied affirmation: Allen v Robles [1969] 1 WLR 1193. Affirmation of the contract can be implied. Thus, if the innocent party calls on the guilty party for further performance of the contract, he will normally be taken to have affirmed the contract since his conduct is only consistent with the continued existence of the contractual obligation. Moreover, if the innocent party himself does acts which are only consistent with the continued existence of the contract, such acts will normally show affirmation of the contract. However, if the innocent party further performs the contract to a*

[1] [1978] ICR 221

[2] [1981] IRLR 443

> *limited extent but at the same time makes it clear that he is reserving his rights to accept the repudiation or is only continuing so as to allow the guilty party to remedy the breach, such further performance does not prejudice his right subsequently to accept the repudiation ..."*

In *Kaur v Leeds Teaching Hospitals NHS Trust*[3] Underhill LJ held at paragraph 51:

> *As I have shown above, both Glidewell LJ in Lewis and Dyson LJ in Omilaju state explicitly that an employee who is the victim of a continuing cumulative breach is entitled to rely on the totality of the employer's acts notwithstanding a prior affirmation; provided the later act forms part of the series (as explained in Omilaju) it does not "land in an empty scale". I do not believe that this involves any tension with the principle that the affirmation of a contract following a breach is irrevocable. Cases of cumulative breach of the Malik term ... fall within the well-recognised qualification to that principle that the victim of a repudiatory breach who has affirmed the contract can nevertheless terminate if the breach continues thereafter. It is true that, as Safehaven says, the correct analysis in such a case is not that the victim can go back on the affirmation and rely on the earlier repudiation as such: rather, the right to terminate depends on the employer's post-affirmation conduct. ...* ***there is nothing wrong in speaking of the right to terminate being revived,*** *by the further act, in the straightforward sense that the employee had the right, then lost it but now has it again.*

[3] [2018] EWCA Civ 978

Waiver

There is a difference between affirmation and waiver. If the employee only affirms the contract, he or she he is still able to sue the employer for damages for the breach of contract. However, if the employee goes further and actually waives the breach, then that right to damages is lost. However, establishing that there has been a waiver of a fundamental breach by an employee will be difficult for an employer to do and following *Kaur* it is possible to revive a waived breach as part of the final straw doctrine, resulting in the employer having to walk on eggshells for the remainder of the employment relationship.

In the case of *Chindove v William Morrisons Supermarket PLC*[4] the Claimant brought two claims: constructive unfair dismissal and direct race discrimination. The ET concluded there had been two acts of direct race discrimination/harassment against the Claimant by a fellow worker. Despite promising to do so, the general manager had not told the Claimant of the outcome of his first informal complaint. A properly considered grievance was rejected, and the claimant complained about the outcome to Head Office. The HR director had purported to carry out further investigation, though she had not in fact done anything much if at all, after a significant delay, and the Claimant resigned 6 weeks later.

Both claims were dismissed. The ET concluded that the resignation was too late for the Claimant to still be entitled to accept the employer's repudiation (which was found as fact) and that the second of the two acts, discrimination/harassment by the fellow worker, occurred 8 months before the claim. It was held that it would not be just and equitable to extend time in respect of the same.

The EAT held that both these decisions were in error because: (1) the ET did not set out its reasons for concluding it was too late, especially

[4] UKEAT/0043/14/BA

since the Claimant was off sick at the time and inferences could not so readily be drawn as to affirmation of the contract where he was not actively working (and it looked as if the ET regarded passage of time alone as sufficient in itself); and (2) the ET had had an argument addressed to it that there was a continuing act/continuum of behaviour, until at least a time within three months of the claim, and had failed altogether to deal with it.

Langstaff J (as he then was) held at paragraphs 24 – 27:

> *24. The context is this. There are two parties to an employment contract. If one, in this case the employer, behaves in a way which shows that it "altogether abandons and refuses to perform the contract", using the most modern formulation of the test, in other words that it will no longer observe its side of the bargain, the employee is left with a choice. He may accept that because the employer is not going to stick to his side of the bargain he, the employee, does not have to do so to his side. If he chooses not to do so, then he will leave employment by resignation, exercising his right to treat himself as discharged. But he may choose instead to go on and to hold his employer to the contract notwithstanding that the employer has indicated he means to break it. The employer remains contractually bound, but in this second scenario, so also does the employee….*
>
> *25. This may have been interpreted as meaning that the passage of time in itself is sufficient for the employee to lose any right to resign. If so, the question might arise what length of time is sufficient? The lay members tell me that there may be an idea in circulation that four weeks is the watershed date. We wish to emphasise that the matter is not one of time in isolation.* ***The principle is whether the employee has demonstrated that he has made the choice. He will do so by conduct; generally by continuing to work in the job from which he need not, if he accepted the employer's repudiation as discharging him from his obligations, have had to do.***

*26. **He may affirm a continuation of the contract in other ways: by what he says, by what he does, by communications which show that he intends the contract to continue. But the issue is essentially one of conduct and not of time.** The reference to time is because if, in the usual case, the employee is at work, then by continuing to work for a time longer than the time within which he might reasonably be expected to exercise his right, he is demonstrating by his conduct that he does not wish to do so. But there is no automatic time; all depends upon the context. Part of that context is the employee's position. As JacobLJ observed in the case of Buckland v Bournemouth University Higher Education Corporation [2010] EWCA Civ 121, deciding to resign is for many, if not most, employees a serious matter. It will require them to give up a job which may provide them with their income, their families with support, and be a source of status to him in his community. His mortgage, his regular expenses, may depend upon it and his economic opportunities for work elsewhere may be slim. There may, on the other hand, be employees who are far less constrained, people who can quite easily obtain employment elsewhere, to whom those considerations do not apply with the same force. It would be entirely unsurprising if the first took much longer to decide on such a dramatic life change as leaving employment which had been occupied for some eight or nine or ten years than it would be in the latter case, particularly if the employment were of much shorter duration. In other words, it all depends upon the context and not upon any strict time test.*

*27. **An important part of the context is whether the employee was actually at work, so that it could be concluded that he was honouring his contract and continuing to do so in a way which was inconsistent with his deciding to go. Where an employee is sick and not working, that observation has nothing like the same force.** We are told, and it is consistent with our papers, that the Claimant here was off sick. Six weeks for a Warehouse Operative, who had worked for eight or nine years in a steady job for a large*

> *company, is a very short time in which to infer from his conduct that he had decided not to exercise his right to go. All the more so, since there seems, on the short findings of fact of this Tribunal, that there was no reason other than the employer's conduct towards him for his choosing to go. We simply cannot say whether this Tribunal had in mind these necessary factors. It did not set out the law. It did not set out the facts which caused it to apply the law. It did not honour rule 30(6). It did not deal with the detailed statement which the Claimant produced in respect of his constructive dismissal though this may be unduly critical of the Tribunal's judgment. The reference to time looks as though the Tribunal simply thought that the passage of time was sufficient in itself. The decision is, effectively, unreasoned.*

In the civil courts, a more robust approach is taken on the issue of delay. In *Brown & Anor v Neon Management Services Ltd & Anor (Rev 1),*[5] the Claimants sought damages and declarations that they were wrongfully dismissed, with the effect that contractual post-termination restrictions ("PTRs") fall away in accordance with the principles established in *General Bill posting Ltd v Atkinson*[6]. Choudhury J stated:

> *"3. In my judgment, it is clear that by resigning on notice on 16 March, Mr Brown and Ms Bhoma affirmed their contracts of employment.* ***It is well-established that in the face of a repudiatory breach of contract the employee must not leave it too long before resigning otherwise he will be taken to have affirmed:*** *see Western Excavating v Sharp [1978] QB 761 (CA) at 769C–D, per Lord Denning MR. In the present case, whilst Mr Brown and Ms Bhoma did reserve all their rights, they clearly indicated that they would be working out the entirety of their notice periods, which, in Mr Brown's case, involved a further year of employment. It would be unconscionable to keep one's right to discharge a repu-*

[5] [2018] EWHC 2137 (QB) (10 August 2018)
[6] [1909] AC 118

> *diated contract alive for that length of time in the absence of any further breaches of contract.* ***Of course, if there are further breaches of contract then, as per the judgment of the Court of Appeal in Kaur, such breaches would not "land in an empty scale" and may be taken into account*** *with the pre-16 March 2018 breaches..."*

The EAT case of *Cockram v Air Products Plc*[7] assessed the position of delay in the context of unfair dismissal claims. The Claimant resigned from his employment in response to what he considered to be a fundamental breach by the Respondent of the implied term of trust and confidence, but he gave 7 months' notice rather than the 3 months required by his contract.

Simler J (as she then was) stated at paragraphs 13 and 14:

> *13. This approach represents the common law contractual approach: a party cannot affirm the contract for a limited period of time and then abrogate it on the expiry of that period of time at common law.* ***At common law therefore, an employee wishing to resign and successfully claim constructive dismissal would have to resign without notice. To do otherwise would be to affirm that part of the contract covered by the period of notice,*** *whilst disaffirming the rest in the sense of accepting the employer's repudiatory conduct as entitling the employee to bring the contract to an immediate end.*
>
> *14. Section 95(1)(c) provides an* ***express statutory exception to this principle by providing for termination of the contract by the employee "with or without notice".*** *In Western Excavating v. Sharp at 768E Lord Denning suggested that: "the words 'with or' were inserted because it was realised that [paragraph 95(1)(c)] as*

[7] UKEAT/0038/14

> *enacted in 1965 left a gap. A man who was considerate enough to give notice was worse off than one who left without notice."*

It was re-iterated that section 95(1)(c) of the Employment Rights Act 1996 varies the common law position by preventing the giving of notice when resigning from being automatically an affirmation of the contract.

Nonetheless, Simler J held that the concept of affirmation remained relevant to the statutory question of whether there had been a constructive dismissal (as defined by section 95(1)(c) ERA). This would always be a fact sensitive question, and there was no rule that post-resignation conduct (such as working a long notice period) was excluded from consideration.

The Claimant had, for his own financial reasons, given a longer notice period than was contractually required, and had thereby affirmed the contract. His constructive unfair dismissal claim was therefore struck out.

Working under protest

In *Buckland v Bournemouth University Higher Education Corporation*[8], the Court of Appeal concluded that a repudiation cannot be cured by the guilty party. At paragraphs 40 and 43, Sedley LJ stated that once a fundamental breach has occurred, "*all the cards are in the hand of the wronged party*" and "*the option of acceptance or affirmation [is] in the innocent party's hands*". At paragraph 52, Jacobs LJ said "[*The employee] should have a clear choice: affirm or go. Of course the wrongdoer can try to make amends – to persuade the wronged party to affirm the contract. But the option ought to be entirely at the wronged party's choice.*"

[8] [2010] EWCA Civ 121

Considering *Buckland* and the judgment of Langstaff J at paragraph 24 of *Chindove*, it is clear that the resignation must occur immediately after the breach of contract or, at the very least, as soon as possible after it.

However, an employee can continue to work following a breach and seek to claim they were constructively dismissed as long as they advise their employer that they are working under protest. If, for example, an employee's contract has changed fundamentally and they disagree with that, rather than resign immediately they are entitled to work under protest until any grievance they have raised regarding the issue has been dealt with. If the grievance does not resolve the position they would then be entitled to resign having worked under protest prior to that date.

Electing to end the contract

The majority of the Supreme Court in *Geys v Societe Generale*[9] held that the elective theory of termination applies to contracts of employment, so that the innocent party must accept a repudiatory breach in order for the contract to come to an end. It does not automatically terminate upon the repudiatory breach.

It was held that the Defendant wrongfully repudiated the contract. The Claimant was employed from 9 February 2005. He had a written contract and further terms were incorporated into it from a handbook. Under the contract, the Claimant's employment could be terminated 'on the expiry of three months' written notice of termination' by either party. The handbook contained a payment in lieu of notice (PILON) clause reserving the Defendant's right to terminate the Claimant's employment 'at any time with immediate effect by making a payment to you in lieu of notice'. If employment was terminated by the Defendant, the Claimant would be entitled to a termination payment,

---

[9] [2012] UKSC 63

calculated by reference to the date of termination of the contract. If the date was after 31 December 2007, the calculation would take into account bonus awards made to the Claimant in 2006 and 2007. If it was before that date, the amount would reflect awards made to the Claimant in 2005 and 2006, which were significantly lower.

On 29 November 2007, the Claimant was called to a meeting given a letter stating that his employment was terminated 'with immediate effect', and was then escorted from the building. On 18 December 2007, the Defendant paid the sums due to the Claimant under the PILON clause into his bank account, which the Claimant became aware of at some point before the end of the year. Nonetheless, the Claimant's solicitor wrote to the Defendant on 2 January 2008 stating that the Claimant had decided to affirm his contract and requesting further details on the compensation and associated payments. The Defendant responded by letter on 4 January 2008, which was deemed to be received by the Claimant on 6 January 2008. This letter made it clear that the Defendant was purporting to dismiss under the PILON clause and that this was the reason for the payment. The Claimant claimed damages for breach of contract and disputed the amount of the termination payment owed to him. Therefore, the Court had to determine the date upon which the Claimant's contract terminated.

The High Court held that, in the absence of a clear agreement between the parties, the contract could not be terminated simply by payment of a sum of money. The Defendant needed to give notice to the Claimant in writing that it was exercising its right under the PILON clause. Accordingly, it held that the Claimant's employment terminated under this clause on 6 January 2008, the first date upon which the Defendant properly notified the Claimant that it had exercised its contractual termination rights. The Court also rejected the Defendant's argument that the Claimant had impliedly accepted its repudiation of contract in purporting to dismiss him with immediate effect on 29 November 2007.

On appeal, the Defendant raised the argument that the contract terminated automatically at the time of its repudiatory breach. Considering itself bound by *Gunton v Richmond-upon-Thames London Borough Council*[10], the Court of Appeal rejected this argument. However, it held that under the PILON clause, the payment was capable of terminating the contract without the Claimant needing to be notified. Therefore, it concluded that the contract terminated on 18 December 2007 when the payment was made into the Claimant's account. The Claimant appealed against this decision and the Defendant appealed against the Court's rejection of the automatic theory of repudiation.

The Supreme Court definitively held that a repudiatory breach only terminates a contract if and when the innocent party elects to accept the breach. The Judgment at Lord Hope at paragraphs 90 – 94 addresses this. This being the 'elective theory' of termination by repudiation, a principle applied to an employment contract by the Court of Appeal in *Gunton*. There has been significant debate over the years as to whether *Gunton* was correct and it had been suggested that repudiatory breach automatically terminates an employment contract without need for acceptance by the innocent party (the 'automatic theory'). The *Geys* case has ended the debate in this regard.

Employee breach of contract predating the employer breach

When considering both an employees and employers breach, *RDF Media Group PLC and another v Clements*[11] held that an employee's previous breach will prevent it from accepting an employer's breach. Consequently, an employee cannot rely on the breach to claim constructive dismissal if they first acted in breach of trust and confidence. Livesey QC stated at paragraph 120:

---

[10] [1981] Ch 448

[11] [2007] EWHC 2892 (QBD) at paragraph 120

> *"…when evaluating whether the employer has breached the implied obligation, it is not unimportant to consider the state of the relationship, which is of course a relationship which both parties have a mutual obligation to foster, at the time when the breach is alleged to have taken place. If, by way of example, an employee has no relationship or is himself in repudiatory breach of his relationship, this may have to be put into the scales as it may affect the balance which has to be struck."*

<u>Delay</u>

In *Chindove v William Morrisons Supermarket Plc*[12] the EAT looked at whether an employee's delay in resignation is fatal to a claim for repudiatory breach of contract.

The Claimant made a complaint to the Respondent in relation to race discrimination but was not told the outcome of his complaint. After a second incident involving the same colleague, the Claimant raised a grievance, which was rejected. He complained about the outcome to the Head Office under a 'special complaint' procedure but the complaint was sent back to the local office. The Claimant went off sick for 6 weeks then resigned. He brought an ET claim for unfair constructive dismissal and race discrimination.

The ET dismissed both claims on the basis that the Claimant's resignation was given too late for him to be entitled to accept the employer's repudiation (which it found as fact). The second act by the colleague was 8 months before the claim and it would not be just and equitable to extend the time. The Claimant appealed. The EAT allowed the appeal on both grounds on the basis that the test for constructive dismissal is one of conduct, not time, and inferences regarding delay in resigning cannot be drawn so easily when an employee is on sick leave.

---

12 [2014] UKEAT/0201/13/BA

The EAT found the ET erred in the following:

1) The ET did not set out its reasons for concluding it was too late, especially since the Claimant was off sick at the time and inferences could not so readily be drawn as to affirmation of the contract where he was not actively working. The ET seemed to regard the passage of time alone as sufficient.

2) The ET failed to address the argument that there was a continuing act/behaviour that went into the 3-month time limit of claim.

CHAPTER ELEVEN

RESIGNATION AND KNOWLEDGE OF BREACH

Forced resignation

Issues may arise in respect of pressure placed by the employer on an employee to resign. An employer may indicate that an employee should resign or they will be sacked, to avoid disciplinary finding and adverse reference. Depending on the facts of the case Courts and Tribunals can conclude that there was an actual dismissal by an employer or alternatively a constructive dismissal. If an employer pressurises an employee to resign this could constitute a breach of the implied term of trust and confidence entitling the employee to resign and claim constructive unfair dismissal. However, when assessing whether there is a dismissal (actual or constructive) it is necessary to interrogate whether there is negotiation leading to a genuine resignation, meaning there is no dismissal.

In the Court of Appeal case of *Sandu v Jan De Ruk Transport Ltd*[1] Mr Sandhu was employed in the London office as an operations manager. He was asked to attend a meeting at the head office in the Netherlands on 6 December 2002. He was not told in advance what that meeting was about. It was clear that the meeting opened with Mr Sandhu being told that he was being dismissed.

The respondent proposed that Mr Sandhu's employment should finish at the end of December 2002. Mr Sandhu negotiated an agreement that he should remain employed until 31 March 2003, that he should retain use of his company car until the end of January 2003, and that he

[1] [2007] IRLR 519, CA

would retain use of his mobile phone, albeit paying for the calls himself from 9 December 2002.

Mr Sandhu brought a claim in the employment tribunal for unfair dismissal. The respondent conceded that had Mr Sandhu left the meeting after hearing the opening remark to the effect that he was being dismissed: (a) he would have been dismissed by the respondent; and (b) the dismissal would have been procedurally unfair. The respondent's case, however, was that it did not dismiss Mr Sandhu; what happened was that, having negotiated satisfactory severance terms during the course of the meeting, Mr Sandhu resigned. The employment tribunal accepted that argument, and rejected Mr Sandhu's complaint. The EAT dismissed Mr Sandhu's appeal against that decision. However, the Court of Appeal allowed the appeal. It held that the EAT had been wrong to uphold the employment tribunal's decision that Mr Sandhu had resigned and had misdirected itself to the law. Had it directed itself properly, the only conclusion which it could properly have reached was that Mr Sandhu had been dismissed. The case was remitted the case for hearing before a different tribunal as to the merits of the unfair dismissal claim.

LJ Wall summarised the legal issues from the leading cases in this context at paragraphs 41 and 44 of the decision. He stated:

> *41 InStaffordshire County Council v Donovan[1981] IRLR 108, Mrs Donovan was an assistant principal planning officer who was subject to ongoing disciplinary proceedings which were themselves subject to a right of appeal on her part. Mrs Donovan was represented in those proceedings by her union organiser and the union solicitor. They negotiated terms on her behalf whereby she was allowed to resign at the end of six months on terms as to payment and the provision of an appropriate testimonial. The EAT, unsurprisingly, held that she had not been dismissed by the county council, but had resigned. As the IRLR headnote puts it:*

*'**If an employee resigns upon being told that unless he resigns he will be dismissed, that is a dismissal in law.** In the present case, however, **the agreement which formed the basis of the employee's resignation was not arrived at under duress and there was no threat of dismissal. The disciplinary proceedings were continuing subject to a right of appeal.***

Where the parties are seeking to negotiate in the course of disciplinary proceedings and an agreed form of resignation is worked out, it would be most unfortunate if the fact that that agreement was reached in the course of disciplinary proceedings entitled the employee thereafter to say that there was a dismissal.'

44 Giving the leading judgment in [Jones v Mid-Glamorgan County Council[1997] IRLR 685CA], Waite LJ examined the law relating to what he described in paragraph 6 of his judgment as 'dismissal by enforced resignation':

*'Courts and tribunals have been willing, from the earliest days of the unfair dismissal jurisdiction, to look, when presented with an apparent resignation, at the substance of the termination for the purpose of inquiring whether the degree of pressure placed on the employee by the employer to retire amounted in reality to a dismissal. In the instant case, the employee had framed his claim in constructive dismissal, and the industrial tribunal dealt with it upon that footing. There was accordingly some discussion before us as to **whether the principle I have just mentioned is to be regarded as deriving from an inference of circumstances giving rise to a constructive dismissal under s.95(1)(c) of the Employment Rights Act 1996, or whether it is more broadly based as a species of direct dismissal.** For my own part, while tending to favour the latter view, I **do not find it necessary to resolve that question in the present case because the principle itself (whatever its origins) is well settled. It is a principle of the utmost flexibility which is willing in all instances of apparent***

> ***voluntary retirement to recognise a dismissal when it sees it, but is by no means prepared to assume that every resignation influenced by pressure or inducement on the part of the employer falls to be so treated. At one end of the scale is the blatant instance of a resignation preceded by the employer's ultimatum: "Retire on my terms or be fired" – where it would not be surprising to find the industrial tribunal drawing the inference that what had occurred was a dismissal. At the other extreme is the instance of the long-serving employee who is attracted to early retirement by benevolent terms of severance offered by grateful employers as a reward for loyalty – where one would expect the industrial tribunal to draw the contrary inference of termination by mutual agreement. Between those two extremes there are bound to lie much more debatable cases to which, according to their particular circumstances, the industrial tribunals are required to apply their expertise in determining whether the borderline has been crossed between a resignation that is truly voluntary and a retirement unwillingly made in response to a threat.*** *I doubt myself whether, given the infinite variety of circumstance, there can be much scope for assistance from authority in discharging that task: indeed, attempts to draw analogies from other cases may provide more confusion than guidance. In cases where precedent is nevertheless thought to be of value, the authority that will no doubt continue to be cited is Sheffield v Oxford Controls Co Ltd [1979] IRLR 133.'LJ Waite paragraph 6*

Communicating reasons

It is obviously preferable for an employee to raise a grievance and specify the reasons for resignation, and employees who fail to do so may face unnecessary evidential difficulties in establishing their case. It was also previously considered that there was a need to notify the employers of the reasons for the acceptance of a repudiation and that an acceptance of a repudiation must be clear and unqualified (*Holland v*

Glendale Industries Ltd[2] and *Norwest Holst Group Administration Ltd v Harrison*[3]). However, the Court of Appeal in *Weathersfield Ltd (T/a Van & Truck Rentals) v Sargeant*[4] addressed the issue of communication of the reasons for resignation.

On 11 April 1996, the Respondent, Mrs. Sargent, who was a young woman, entered the employment of the Appellants as a receptionist. She was given an instruction that cars and vans should not be rented out to Asian or coloured people. She was given a further similar instruction on Friday 12 April 1996. She made no immediate protest, but, over the following weekend she decided that she could not comply with the instructions that she had been given and on Monday 15 April 1996, she telephoned the employers and told them that she could not do the job. The employers were informed of the reason why she left by letter on 18 April 1996.

Pill LJ stated at paragraph 20:

> ***I reject as a proposition of law the notion that there can be no acceptance of a repudiation unless the employee tells the employer, at the time, that he is leaving because of the employer's repudiatory conduct.*** *Each case will turn on its own facts and, where no reason is communicated to the employer at the time, the fact finding tribunal may more readily conclude that the repudiatory conduct was not the reason for the employee leaving. In each case it will, however, be for the fact finding tribunal, considering all the evidence, to decide whether there has been an acceptance.*

Swinton Thomas LJ stated at paragraph 31:

---

[2] [1998] ICR 493

[3] [1985] ICR 668

[4] [1999] IRLR 94

> *I agree with Pill, L.J. that there is no requirement as a matter of law that an employee must state his reason for leaving although a failure to do so may make it more difficult to establish constructive dismissal.*

Assessing the reason for resignation

When assessing what is actually the reason for resignation it is necessary to assess whether the fundamental breach of contract '*played a part in the dismissal'*.

In *Wright v North Ayrshire Council*[5] the EAT considered an appeal against the ET's decision that the Claimant had not been unfairly constructively dismissed.

The Claimant worked shifts as a care at home assistant. She brought grievances against the Respondent which were not dealt with properly. She then went through a very difficult period when her mother died and her partner suffered a stroke, and split shifts did not make it easy to cope with this situation. Attempts to reorganise her working pattern appear not to have been successful.

The Claimant resigned and claimed constructive unfair dismissal. The ET rejected her claim. She passed the first two stages of a constructive dismissal claim but the ET ruled that the effective cause of her resignation was not the repudiation of her contract but because she could not cope with the demands of her job while her partner was ill. They said *'The Tribunal has already indicated that where a Tribunal believe there may be more than one reason why an employee leaves a job, the correct approach is to ask what was the effective cause of the resignatio*n'.

The EAT allowed the appeal. The ET had only referred to the case of*Jones v Sirl*and interpreted it incorrectly as saying that where there is

[5] UKEATS/0017/13

more than one cause it is only the main, principal, and in that sense effective, cause which it should be looking for. So where there is a mixture of motives, as the ET put it here, a Tribunal must determine which is the effective cause of the resignation. Langstaff J held at paragraph 18 that this finding was wrong; the search was not for one cause which predominated over others, or which would on its own be sufficient, but to ask (as Elias J put it in*Abbey Cars v Ford*) whether the repudiatory breach **'played a part in the dismissal'**. The appeal was allowed and remitted to the same Tribunal.

<u>Knowledge of breach</u>

Knowledge of the breach of contract during the employment relationship is not necessary to found a claim for the breach of the implied term of trust and confidence. The question of when the breach is discovered is highly relevant to remedies because if the breach is not discovered until after the employment ends, the employee could obviously not rely upon this as a ground for terminating the contract and it would therefore provide no basis for an unfair dismissal claim. Breaches discovered after termination could however be relied on to seek to prevent an employer enforcing post termination restrictions.

In the case of *Malik and another v Bank of Credit and Commerce International SA*[6] it was held that knowledge of the breach is not essential. Lord Steyn stated at paragraph 61:

> "... ***there is nothing heterodox about allowing a claim for damages for a breach occurring during the contractual relationship where damage resulting from the breach only becomes manifest after the termination of the relationship***. *In truth the ignorance of an employee of a breach of the implied obligation is*

[6] [1997] IRLR 462

> *only relevant to the choice of remedies: obviously the employee cannot decide to terminate on a ground of which he is unaware."*[7]

Lord Nicholls stated at paragraphs 18 – 20 of *Malik*:

> *"18 In the nature of things, the remedy of treating the conduct as a repudiatory breach, entitling the employee to leave, can only avail an employee who learns of the facts while still employed. If he does not discover the facts while his employment is still continuing, perforce this remedy is not open to him. But this does not mean he has no remedy. In the ordinary course breach of a contractual term entitles the innocent party to damages.*
>
> *Remedies: (2) damages*
>
> *19 Can an employee recover damages for breach of the trust and confidence term when he first learns of the breach after he has left the employment? The answer to this question is inextricably bound up with the further question of what damages are recoverable for a breach of this term. In turn, the answer to this further question is inextricably linked with one aspect of the decision in Addis v Gramophone Co Ltd [1909] AC 488.*
>
> *20 At first sight, it seems almost a contradiction in terms that an employee can suffer recoverable loss if he first learns of the trust-destroying conduct after the employment contract has already ended for other reasons. But of the many forms which trust-destroying conduct may take, some may have continuing adverse financial effects on an employee even after his employment has ceased. In such a case, the fact that the employee only learned of the employer's conduct after the employment had ended ought not, in principle, to be a bar to recovery. If it were otherwise, an employer who conceals a breach would be better placed than an employer who does not."*

---

[7] Per Lord Steyn paragraph 61; 110 RDF Livesey QC (QB)

In the High Court case of *RDF Media Group Plc and or v Alan Clements*[8] Per Livesey QC, sitting as a Judge of the High Court, stated at paragraph 110:

> *"110 As a matter of practicality these observations are of course absolutely correct. However, it seems also to be the case that, as a matter of principle, an employee who claims constructive dismissal on the grounds of breach of the implied obligation may, if he fails to establish the breach on which he purported to claim that his employment ended, rely on any matters constituting a breach which he has discovered only since he resigned. This seems to follow from the application of general contractual principles laid down in the case of Boston Deep Sea Fishing and Ice Co v Ansell (1888) 39 Ch.D 339. The employer in that case was not able to establish at trial the grounds on which it had dismissed Mr Ansell but was entitled to rely on a separate breach which it had discovered only thereafter."*

Ignorance of rights

Employees frequently rely upon breach of statutory rights, such as failure to pay minimum wage, breach of Equality Act 2010 provisions or detrimental treatment following raising discrimination complaints or protected disclosures for whistleblowing complaints.

In the case of *Mruke v Khan*[9], the Court of Appeal considered the issue of whether there can be a repudiatory breach of contract on account of less favourable treatment where the employee is ignorant of his or her rights.

The Claimant was a 54-year-old illiterate Tanzanian national who had been employed by the Respondent as a domestic worker. She previously

[8] [2007] EWHC 2892 (QB)
[9] [2018] EWCA Civ 280

worked at a hospital in Tanzania run by the Respondent. She came to the UK in 2006 and worked in the Respondent's home until 2010 when she left the employment.

The ET allowed her claims for unlawful deduction of wages, arising from the Respondent's failure to pay her the national minimum wage rate, holiday pay or give proper rest breaks. The ET dismissed her claims for race discrimination and constructive unfair dismissal. The ET found that she had not been treated less favourably than a hypothetical comparator. Whilst failure to pay minimum wage was a repudiatory breach, the Claimant had not known she was entitled to minimum wage and had not resigned in response to that breach. The EAT dismissed her appeal.

The Court of Appeal allowed the subsequent appeal in part on the basis that the ET erred in its approach regarding her claim for constructive unfair dismissal (which was based on the employer's failure to pay national minimum wage). The fact that the Claimant had been unaware of her entitlement to minimum wage did not prevent the failure amounting to a repudiatory breach of contract. There was evidence that the Claimant asserted that she had not been paid and was on 'minimal pay' and this was part of the factual basis of her resignation. Singh LJ considered that this was one of the rare cases where the ET decision was perverse on the evidence before it.

CHAPTER TWELVE

CONSTRUCTIVE UNFAIR DISMISSAL

Constructive dismissal is a breach of contract claim. Consequently, the only damages available to the employee claiming constructive dismissal are those sums which are due under the terms of the employment contract. If the employee has resigned without notice that will usually be just the employee's notice pay or other contractual benefits during the notice period. The employee does not need any particular length of service to claim constructive dismissal.

However, an unfair constructive dismissal arises from the Employment Rights Act 1996 and, pursuant to section 108, generally applies to employees with two years' continuous service. There are a number of 'automatic unfair' dismissals where two years' service is not required, including dismissals for family leave reasons, health and safety, whistleblowing and asserting a statutory right.

If the tribunal finds the employer liable for constructive dismissal, the finding of unfair dismissal will often follow. However, it is open to the employer to show that such dismissal was for a potentially fair reason. If the employer does so, it will then be for the Tribunal to decide whether dismissal for that reason, both substantively and procedurally, fell within the range of reasonable responses and was fair.

For example, an employer may cut the employee's contractual hours. This is a repudiatory breach of contract and in those circumstances the employee would win his constructive dismissal claim. However, the employer may argue that it cut the hours for a genuine business reason, such as a downturn in trade, and in those circumstances the dismissal was potentially fair. The employee would succeed with the constructive dismissal claim for notice pay but may lose the unfair element of the claim.

In the EAT case of *Argos Ltd v Ms K Kuldo*[1] the Respondent employer appealed against a judgment holding that the Claimant had been unfairly dismissed. In a restructuring exercise the Respondent had sought to "map" the Claimant into a new role and did not treat her as redundant. The Claimant resigned in protest, claiming constructive unfair dismissal, wrongful dismissal and a redundancy payment. The ET found that the new role was significantly different to the old role, and that the Respondent had breached the implied term of trust and confidence when it failed to consult, failed to properly assess the roles and failed to properly address the Claimant's grievance and appeal. The ET committed no error of law in finding that the Claimant was constructively dismissed. Its overall conclusion and findings of fact were not perverse. However, in finding that the dismissal was unfair, the ET failed to direct itself that this was a separate issue, failed to address the issue of reason for dismissal and fairness and/or failed to give proper reasons for its conclusion that the dismissal was unfair. The ET erred in law to that extent, but that error did not undermine the finding of constructive dismissal.

Under section 111 of the Employment Rights Act 1996, complaints for unfair constructive dismissal claims must be presented to the Tribunal within three months less one day of the date the employment contract terminated. This time limit may be extended under the compulsory ACAS Early Conciliation procedure.

Under section 124 of the Employment Rights Act 1996, there is a maximum compensatory award of £88,519, or 52 weeks gross salary, whichever is the lower. The compensatory cap is subject to an annual inflationary increase.

---

[1] UKEAT/0225/19/BA

For high earning employees with long contractual notice periods it is more advantageous for a claim for breach of contract to be brought in the civil courts because at present damages for breach of contract claims in the employment tribunal are limited to £25,000.The time limit to submit a claim in the civil court for breach of contract is six years. These anomalous differences have been the subject of the recent Law Commission report https://www.lawcom.gov.uk/project/employment-law-hearing-structures/ and proposals have been made to bring consistency between worker contract claims in the Employment Tribunal and the County Court.

CHAPTER THIRTEEN

TUPE

TUPE provides that if employees transfer, they will transfer automatically on the same terms and conditions[1]. However, employees have a choice, and have the right to object to the transfer if they wish.

If an employee objects to a TUPE transfer they are taken to have resigned, with effect from the date of the transfer, and do not have any legal remedy, save in very limited circumstances provided by Regulation 4(9) TUPE 2006.

Where an employee's employment transfers under TUPE, Regulation 4 (9) allows an employee to resign and treat themselves as constructively dismissed where the transfer involves or will involve:

- a substantial change;
- in the employee's working conditions;
- to their material detriment; and
- liability for the employee's claim will usually rest with the new service provider.

A "substantial change to working conditions" is more than just a proposed change to terms and conditions of employment. The term "working conditions" is used, which is broader, extending to non-contractual matters such as uniform, reporting lines and non-contractual benefits. A material detriment does not necessarily have to be so serious as to amount to a repudiatory breach of contract such as in the case of

---

[1] TUPE 2006 Regulations – See Appendix B

constructive dismissal, but the change must have a significant impact on the employee and must not be trivial.

A change in the identity of the employer could constitute a "substantial change", for example if the employee would suffer a loss in status or the identity of the employer has a stigma that runs contrary to the principles of the employee or could have a prejudicial effect on the employees future job prospects.

It is questionable whether a mobility clause can extend to allowing employees to be moved from locations operated by the transferor to allow a transferee to move the employees to their own sites. However, where there is a general mobility clause this may be permitted within the scope of contract, provided that the transferee implements this change with reasonable notice and with due regard to the impact on the employees.

In addition to regulation 4(9), transferred employees may also consider resigning and claim constructive dismissal under TUPE if the move is significant and likely to cause them a material detriment. Therefore, an element of caution is required when implementing changes to working conditions in the context of a TUPE transfer.

In the case of *Tapere v South London and Maudsley NHS Trust*[2] the EAT considered material detriment under Regulation 4(9) TUPE 2006, which allows an employee to treat themselves as constructively dismissed where a TUPE transfer involves or will involve a substantial change to their working conditions which causes them a material detriment.

HHJ Hand QC held that whether there is a substantial change in working conditions is a question of fact, which is to be determined by reference to the nature as well as the degree of change. However, when

---

[2] UKEAT/0410/08

assessing whether or not a particular change is to an employee's detriment a subjective approach is required.

Ms Tapere brought such a claim following a transfer of her employment from Lewisham PCT (the "PCT") to the Trust which required a change in her place of work from Camberwell to Beckenham. It was written into her contract that her place of work was the Camberwell site but the contract also contained a "mobility clause" which stated that 'there may be occasions when you are required to perform your duties either temporarily or permanently at other locations within the [PCT]'.

Ms Tapere alleged that this change was substantial and placed her at a detriment in terms of potential disruption to childcare arrangements and a different journey (on the M25) which she did not consider attractive. The Trust maintained that the additional travel time was actually minimal and that they had acted reasonably in agreeing to vary Ms Tapere's start time. The ET dismissed Ms Tapere's claim.

The ET held that Ms Tapere's contract of employment contained a mobility clause which transferred under TUPE so that the Trust could move her within its own geographical location. The Employment Tribunal also concluded that Ms Tapere could not rely upon Regulation 4(9) of TUPE as, viewed objectively, there was not a substantial change to her detriment. Ms Tapere appealed to the EAT.

HHJ Hand QC held that the Trust was not permitted to rely on the mobility clause in Ms Tapere's contract as this could only be construed as to cover locations belonging to the PCT and not the Trust. HHJ Hand QC concluded at paragraph 45:

> *Whether or not there is a change in working conditions will be a simple question of fact. Whether or not it is a change of substance will also be a question of fact and the Employment Tribunal will need to consider the nature as well as the degree of the change in*

> *order to decide whether it is substantial. In the sense that the employee will not be the arbitrator of whether the change is substantial, it might be said that the approach is objective but, as the case of **Merckx and Neuhuys v Ford Motors Belgium SA** illustrates, the character of the change is likely to be the most important aspect of determining whether the change is substantial. There, the European Court of Justice regarded the change as substantial because it was a change in remuneration. No doubt, in such cases there will be endless scope for argument as to the degree of change; the employer will assert that the money will be the same in the end result; the employee will protest that cannot be so; but the focus, in our judgment must be on the nature of the change.*

On the question of detriment, HHJ Hand QC stated at paragraphs 52 to 54 that the Tribunal ought to consider whether the employee in question regarded the consequences of the change as detrimental and if so, whether that was a reasonable position to adopt. However, the detriment must be more than trivial or fanciful.

CHAPTER FOURTEEN

WRONGFUL DISMISSAL AND POST TERMINATION RESTRICTIONS

Many cases are brought in the High Court for constructive dismissal by employees seeking to discharge potentially onerous post termination restrictions (PTRs) in their contracts of employment. It is clear that compelling evidence of breach is required in order to establish this.

In the case of *Tullet Prebon PLC and others v BGC Brokers LP*[1] Mr Verrier was employed as chief operating officer by Tullett. He was Tullett's second most senior executive. He moved to work for BGC as its executive managing director and general manager.

BGC were organised into desks in accordance with the products in which they dealt. A broker's success depended on good relationships with traders. Broker companies such as Tullett and BGC sought to protect themselves from having their successful brokers recruited by a rival. They did so by means of contracts of employment lasting initially for minimum periods of two years or more, after which period the employee could give six or 12 months' notice of termination, with post termination restrictions which would prevent the employee working for a rival for a further period, typically six months. Contracts also commonly contained a garden leave provision.

The device used to recruit employees who had long-term contracts with their existing employers was called a 'forward contract'. The employee would sign a contract with the recruiting company by which he undertook to commence employment with it as soon as he was free to do so. There was likely to be a substantial signing payment on com-

[1] [2011] IRLR 420, CA

mencing. Indemnities could also be given against financial loss arising from the transfer.

Mr Verrier brought into action a plan to recruit Tullett brokers to work for BGC. He sought to recruit whole desks. Thirteen Tullett brokers signed forward contracts to move to BGC. Signing payments and indemnities were given. Three of those brokers later changed their minds. Tullett brought proceedings against BGC, Mr Verrier and BGC's president, Mr Lynn, alleging inducement of breaches of contract, amongst other things. The 10 brokers who had decided to move to BGC were also defendants to the proceedings brought by Tullett. They claimed that they had been constructively dismissed. They argued, amongst other things, that Tullett had breached the implied term of trust and confidence in making threats to sue them if they breached their contracts with it, and in trying to persuade them to stay with it in breach of their forward contracts with BGC. BGC brought a counterclaim against Tullett for allegedly inducing the three brokers who decided to stay at Tullett to breach their forward contracts with BGC.

Then Jack J held, amongst other things, that the 10 brokers had not been constructively dismissed. He considered that Tullett's intention had been to preserve the employment relationships, rather than destroy them. He also held that Tullett was not liable to BGC for inducing the three brokers who had decided to stay with Tullett to breach their forward contracts with BGC. He held that the three brokers had been entitled to repudiate their contracts as BGC's conduct showed a cynical disregard for the law and for employees' duties which amounted to a breach of the obligation of trust and confidence in the forward contracts.

BGC appealed. Amongst other things, it argued that the judge had erred in finding that Tullett was not in breach of the implied term of trust and confidence, as he had impermissibly taken into account Tullett's subjective intentions rather than considering whether Tullett's conduct, objectively considered, constituted a breach of the obligation of trust.

Secondly, it argued that Jack J had erred in rejecting its counterclaim in respect of the three brokers who had stayed with Tullett. It argued that Jack J had been wrong to find BGC in breach of any implied term of trust and confidence to the three brokers, as no such obligation arose in the forward contracts, which were not contracts of employment. It pointed out that at the time the three brokers had been in a relationship of trust and confidence with their current employer, Tullett, which it argued was inconsistent with any such relationship with a prospective employer.

The Court of Appeal dismissed the appeal. In particular, Maurice Kay LJ held at paragraphs 18 – 28:

1 Jack J had not erred in dismissing the allegations of constructive dismissal against Tullett. The question of whether or not there has been a repudiatory breach of the duty of trust and confidence is a *'question of fact for the tribunal of fact'*. It a highly context-specific question.

2 The legal test is whether, looking at all the circumstances objectively, that is from the perspective of a reasonable person in the position of the innocent party, the contract breaker has clearly shown an intention to abandon and altogether refuse to perform the contract. The issue is repudiatory breach in circumstances where the objectively assessed intention of the alleged contract-breaker towards the employees is of a paramount importance. In the present case, the judge had approached the issue correctly. He had not applied a subjective approach. He had objectively assessed the true intention of Tullett and had reached the conclusions that their intention was not to attack but to strengthen the employment relationship. That was a per-

missible and correct finding, reached after a careful consideration of all the circumstances which had to be taken into account insofar as they bore on an objective assessment of the intention of the alleged contract breaker. Further, an employee's conduct might be relevant to whether the employee had breached the implied term.

3 Jack J had not erred in rejecting BGC's counterclaim. Obligations of trust and confidence can arise as appropriate, taking account of the circumstances, before the actual commencement of employment, at a time of detailed contractual regulation between the parties, even though the relationship at that time is not purely and simply one of current employment. In that regard, a contract obliging a person to commence employment at a future date is a contract of employment for the purpose of the jurisdiction of the employment tribunal. The forward contract is more akin to a contract of employment than to a purely commercial agreement. The situation is one in which there is an overarching obligation implied by law as an incident of the contract. The fact of the continuing contracts of employment between the employees and the current employer may attenuate the obligation as between the employees and the prospective employer, but there is no legal or logical inconsistency about the concurrence of the obligations, whatever difference there may be in relation to the respective contents.

4 In the present case, the prospective employer with whom the three brokers had entered into forward contracts was doing its utmost, by illegal and dishonest conduct, to cripple its competitor by which they remained employed. It was difficult to imagine circumstances affording greater justification for prospective employees seeing the conduct of their prospective employer as a repudiatory breach of the

obligation of trust and confidence. As a matter of fact and law, the judge was right to have concluded that BGC had committed repudiatory breaches of the forward contracts, as a result of which the three brokers had committed no breach when terminating their contracts.

5 The conclusion was that the employer's intention may form part of the overall assessment of whether, objectively speaking, there has been a repudiatory breach.

The case of *Square Global Ltd v Leonard*[2] was an employment law dispute in the financial services field. The main issues between the parties was whether the employee was constructively dismissed, and if not, the enforceability of PTR's. At paragraphs 131 – 151 of the judgment, Mr Turner QC, sitting as a Deputy High Court Judge, provides a comprehensive legal analysis of the important constructive dismissal principles. Ultimately, he concluded that the Claimant was not constructively dismissed and the PTR's were enforceable against the Mr Leonard.

In *Brown & Anor v Neon Management Services Ltd & Anor*[3] the Claimants sought damages and declarations that they were wrongfully dismissed, with the effect that contractual PTRs fall away in accordance with the principles established in *General Bill posting Ltd v Atkinson*[4]. The Claimants were successful in both respects.

The Claimants resigned on notice after the Defendant failed to pay salary increases and discretionary bonuses that had been awarded to them, made the salary increases and bonuses conditional upon acceptance of detrimental new contractual terms and removed profit commission ("PC") agreed at the time of their recruitment. The Claimants contended that those breaches individually and cumulatively

---

[2] [2020] EWHC 1008 (QB)

[3] (Rev 1) [2018] EWHC 2137 (QB) (10 August 2018)

[4] [1909] AC 118

amounted to a repudiatory breach of contract entitling them to resign. Thereafter, the Claimants, and in particular the First and Second Claimants, contended that the Defendants committed further repudiatory breaches of contract whereby they accepted that alleged repudiation by resigning with immediate effect on 1 May 2018. They claimed damages and declarations that they were wrongfully dismissed, with the effect that contractual post-termination restrictions fell away.

Choudhury J ruled in their favour in both respects. If there had been no further breaches of contract after the on notice resignations, the Claimants would have affirmed their contracts, the notice periods being 6 months and 12 months. It is well-established that in the face of a repudiatory breach of contract the employee must not leave it too long before resigning otherwise he will be taken to have affirmed. However, in this case, following *Kaur*, there were further breaches of contract entitling the Claimants to resign as a result of the Defendant's conduct, and they acted promptly in so doing.

APPENDIX A

SECTION 1 EMPLOYMENT RIGHTS ACT 1996

Statement of initial employment particulars.

(1) Wherea workerbegins employment with an employer, the employer shall give tothe workera written statement of particulars of employment.

(2) Subject to sections 2(2) to (4)—

(a) the particulars required by subsections (3) and (4) must be included in a single document; and

(b) the statement must be given not later than the beginning of the employment.]

(3) The statement shall contain particulars of—

(a) the names of the employer andworker,

(b) the date when the employment began, and

(c) In the case of a statement given to an employee, the date on which the employee's period of continuous employment began (taking into account any employment with a previous employer which counts towards that period).

(4) The statement shall also contain particulars, as at a specified date not more than seven days before the statement (or the instalment of a statement given under section 2(4) containing them)]is given, of—

(a) the scale or rate of remuneration or the method of calculating remuneration,

(b) the intervals at which remuneration is paid (that is, weekly, monthly or other specified intervals),

(c) any terms and conditions relating to hours of work including any terms and conditions relating to—

(i) normal working hours,

(ii) the days of the week the worker is required to work, and

(iii) whether or not such hours or days may be variable, and if they may be how they vary or how that variation is to be determined.]

(d) any terms and conditions relating to any of the following—

(i) entitlement to holidays, including public holidays, and holiday pay (the particulars given being sufficient to enable theworker'sentitlement, including any entitlement to accrued holiday pay on the termination of employment, to be precisely calculated),

(ii) incapacity for work due to sickness or injury, including any provision for sick pay,..

(iia) any other paid leave, and

(iii) pensions and pension schemes,

(da) any other benefits provided by the employer that do not fall within another paragraph of this subsection,

(e) the length of notice which theworker is obliged to give and entitled to receive to terminate his contract of employmentor other worker's contract,

(f) the title of the job which theworkeris employed to do or a brief description of the work for which he is employed,

(g) where the employment is not intended to be permanent, the period for which it is expected to continue or, if it is for a fixed term, the date when it is to end,

(ga) any probationary period, including any conditions and its duration,]

(h) either the place of work or, where theworker is required or permitted to work at various places, an indication of that and of the address of the employer,

(j) any collective agreements which directly affect the terms and conditions of the employment including, where the employer is not a party, the persons by whom they were made,

(k) where theworkeris required to work outside the United Kingdom for a period of more than one month—

(i) the period for which he is to work outside the United Kingdom,

(ii) the currency in which remuneration is to be paid while he is working outside the United Kingdom,

(iii) any additional remuneration payable to him, and any benefits to be provided to or in respect of him, by reason of his being required to work outside the United Kingdom, and

(iv) any terms and conditions relating to his return to the United Kingdom.

(l) any training entitlement provided by the employer,

(m) any part of that training entitlement which the employer requires the worker to complete, and

(n) any other training which the employer requires the worker to complete and which the employer will not bear the cost of.

(5) Subsection (4)(d)(iii) does not apply toa workerof a body or authority if —

(a) theworker'spension rights depend on the terms of a pension scheme established under any provision contained in or having effect under any Act, and

(b) any such provision requires the body or authority to give to a newworkerinformation concerning theworker'spension rights or the determination of questions affecting those rights.

(6) In this section "probationary period" means a temporary period specified in the contract of employment or other worker's contract between a worker and an employer that—

(a) commences at the beginning of the employment, and

(b) is intended to enable the employer to assess the worker's suitability for the employment.

APPENDIX B

TUPE REGS (EXTRACT)

Relevant regulations of the Transfer of Undertakings (Protection of Employment) Regulations 2006

Effect of relevant transfer on contracts of employment

3.—(1) These Regulations apply to—

(a) a transfer of an undertaking, business or part of an undertaking or business situated immediately before the transfer in the United Kingdom to another person where there is a transfer of an economic entity which retains its identity;

(b) a service provision change, that is a situation in which—

(i) activities cease to be carried out by a person ("a client") on his own behalf and are carried out instead by another person on the client's behalf ("a contractor");

(ii) activities cease to be carried out by a contractor on a client's behalf (whether or not those activities had previously been carried out by the client on his own behalf) and are carried out instead by another person ("a subsequent contractor") on the client's behalf; or

(iii) activities cease to be carried out by a contractor or a subsequent contractor on a client's behalf (whether or not those activities had previously been carried out by the client on his own behalf) and are carried out instead by the client on his own behalf and in which the conditions set out in paragraph (3) are satisfied.

(2) In this regulation "economic entity" means an organised grouping of resources which has the objective of pursuing an economic activity, whether or not that activity is central or ancillary.

(3) The conditions referred to in paragraph (1)(b) are that—

(a) immediately before the service provision change—

(i) there is an organised grouping of employees situated in Great Britain which has as its principal purpose the carrying out of the activities concerned on behalf of the client;

(ii) the client intends that the activities will, following the service provision change, be carried out by the transferee other than in connection with a single specific event or task of short-term duration; and

(b) the activities concerned do not consist wholly or mainly of the supply of goods for the client's use.

(4) Subject to paragraph (1), these Regulations apply to—

(a) public and private undertakings engaged in economic activities whether or not they are operating for gain;

(b) a transfer or service provision change howsoever effected notwithstanding—

(i) that the transfer of an undertaking, business or part of an undertaking or business is governed or effected by the law of a country or territory outside the United Kingdom or that the service provision change is governed or effected by the law of a country or territory outside Great Britain;

(ii) that the employment of persons employed in the undertaking, business or part transferred or, in the case of a service provision change, persons employed in the organised grouping of employees, is governed by any such law;

(c) a transfer of an undertaking, business or part of an undertaking or business (which may also be a service provision change) where persons employed in the undertaking, business or part transferred ordinarily work outside the United Kingdom.

(5) An administrative reorganisation of public administrative authorities or the transfer of administrative functions between public administrative authorities is not a relevant transfer.

(6) A relevant transfer—

(a) may be effected by a series of two or more transactions; and

(b) may take place whether or not any property is transferred to the transferee by the transferor.

(7) Where, in consequence (whether directly or indirectly) of the transfer of an undertaking, business or part of an undertaking or business which was situated immediately before the transfer in the United Kingdom, a ship within the meaning of the Merchant Shipping Act 1995(1) registered in the United Kingdom ceases to be so registered, these Regulations shall not affect the right conferred by section 29 of that Act (right of seamen to be discharged when ship ceases to be registered in the United Kingdom) on a seaman employed in the ship.

Effect of relevant transfer on contracts of employment

4.—(1) Except where objection is made under paragraph (7), a relevant transfer shall not operate so as to terminate the contract of employment of any person employed by the transferor and assigned to the organised grouping of resources or employees that is subject to the relevant transfer, which would otherwise be terminated by the transfer, but any such contract shall have effect after the transfer as if originally made between the person so employed and the transferee.

(2) Without prejudice to paragraph (1), but subject to paragraph (6), and regulations 8 and 15(9), on the completion of a relevant transfer—

(a) all the transferor's rights, powers, duties and liabilities under or in connection with any such contract shall be transferred by virtue of this regulation to the transferee; and

(b) any act or omission before the transfer is completed, of or in relation to the transferor in respect of that contract or a person assigned to that organised grouping of resources or employees, shall be deemed to have been an act or omission of or in relation to the transferee.

(3) Any reference in paragraph (1) to a person employed by the transferor and assigned to the organised grouping of resources or employees that is subject to a relevant transfer, is a reference to a person so employed immediately before the transfer, or who would have been so employed if he had not been dismissed in the circumstances described in regulation 7(1), including, where the transfer is effected by a series of two or more transactions, a person so employed and assigned or who would have been so employed and assigned immediately before any of those transactions.

(4) Subject to regulation 9, in respect of a contract of employment that is, or will be, transferred by paragraph (1), any purported variation of the contract shall be void if the sole or principal reason for the variation is—

(a) the transfer itself; or

(b) a reason connected with the transfer that is not an economic, technical or organisational reason entailing changes in the workforce.

(5) Paragraph (4) shall not prevent the employer and his employee, whose contract of employment is, or will be, transferred by paragraph (1), from agreeing a variation of that contract if the sole or principal reason for the variation is—

(a) a reason connected with the transfer that is an economic, technical or organisational reason entailing changes in the workforce; or

(b) a reason unconnected with the transfer.

(6) Paragraph (2) shall not transfer or otherwise affect the liability of any person to be prosecuted for, convicted of and sentenced for any offence.

(7) Paragraphs (1) and (2) shall not operate to transfer the contract of employment and the rights, powers, duties and liabilities under or in connection with it of an employee who informs the transferor or the transferee that he objects to becoming employed by the transferee.

(8) Subject to paragraphs (9) and (11), where an employee so objects, the relevant transfer shall operate so as to terminate his contract of employment with the transferor but he shall not be treated, for any purpose, as having been dismissed by the transferor.

(9) Subject to regulation 9, where a relevant transfer involves or would involve a substantial change in working conditions to the material detriment of a person whose contract of employment is or would be transferred under paragraph (1), such an employee may treat the contract of employment as having been terminated, and the employee shall be treated for any purpose as having been dismissed by the employer.

(10) No damages shall be payable by an employer as a result of a dismissal falling within paragraph (9) in respect of any failure by the employer to pay wages to an employee in respect of a notice period which the employee has failed to work.

(11) Paragraphs (1), (7), (8) and (9) are without prejudice to any right of an employee arising apart from these Regulations to terminate his contract of employment without notice in acceptance of a repudiatory breach of contract by his employer.

'A Practical Guide to the Pre-Action RTA Claims Protocol for Personal Injury Lawyers' by Antonia Ford
'A Practical Guide to Neighbour Disputes and the Law' by Alexander Walsh
'A Practical Guide to Forfeiture of Leases' by Mark Shelton
'A Practical Guide to Coercive Control for Legal Practitioners and Victims' by Rachel Horman
'A Practical Guide to Rights Over Airspace and Subsoil' by Daniel Gatty
'Tackling Disclosure in the Criminal Courts – A Practitioner's Guide' by Narita Bahra QC & Don Ramble
'A Practical Guide to the Law of Driverless Cars – Second Edition' by Alex Glassbrook, Emma Northey & Scarlett Milligan
'A Practical Guide to TOLATA Claims' by Greg Williams
'Artificial Intelligence – The Practical Legal Issues' by John Buyers
'A Practical Guide to the Law of Prescription in Scotland' by Andrew Foyle
'A Practical Guide to the Construction and Rectification of Wills and Trust Instruments' by Edward Hewitt
'A Practical Guide to the Law of Bullying and Harassment in the Workplace' by Philip Hyland
'How to Be a Freelance Solicitor: A Practical Guide to the SRA-Regulated Freelance Solicitor Model' by Paul Bennett
'A Practical Guide to Prison Injury Claims' by Malcolm Johnson
'A Practical Guide to the Small Claims Track' by Dominic Bright
'A Practical Guide to Advising Clients at the Police Station' by Colin Stephen McKeown-Beaumont
'A Practical Guide to Antisocial Behaviour Injunctions' by Iain Wightwick
'Practical Mediation: A Guide for Mediators, Advocates, Advisers, Lawyers, and Students in Civil, Commercial, Business, Property, Workplace, and Employment Cases' by Jonathan Dingle with John Sephton
'The Mini-Pupillage Workbook' by David Boyle

'A Practical Guide to Crofting Law' by Brian Inkster
'A Practical Guide to Spousal Maintenance' by Liz Cowell
'A Practical Guide to the Law of Domain Names and Cybersquatting' by Andrew Clemson
'A Practical Guide to the Law of Gender Pay Gap Reporting' by Harini Iyengar
'A Practical Guide to the Rights of Grandparents in Children Proceedings' by Stuart Barlow
'NHS Whistleblowing and the Law' by Joseph England
'Employment Law and the Gig Economy' by Nigel Mackay & Annie Powell
'A Practical Guide to Noise Induced Hearing Loss (NIHL) Claims' by Andrew Mckie, Ian Skeate, Gareth McAloon
'An Introduction to Beauty Negligence Claims – A Practical Guide for the Personal Injury Practitioner' by Greg Almond
'Intercompany Agreements for Transfer Pricing Compliance' by Paul Sutton
'Zen and the Art of Mediation' by Martin Plowman
'A Practical Guide to the SRA Principles, Individual and Law Firm Codes of Conduct 2019 – What Every Law Firm Needs to Know' by Paul Bennett
'A Practical Guide to Adoption for Family Lawyers' by Graham Pegg
'A Practical Guide to Industrial Disease Claims' by Andrew Mckie & Ian Skeate
'A Practical Guide to Redundancy' by Philip Hyland
'A Practical Guide to Vicarious Liability' by Mariel Irvine
'A Practical Guide to Applications for Landlord's Consent and Variation of Leases' by Mark Shelton
'A Practical Guide to Relief from Sanctions Post-Mitchell and Denton' by Peter Causton
'A Practical Guide to Equity Release for Advisors' by Paul Sams
'A Practical Guide to Unlawful Eviction and Harassment' by Stephanie Lovegrove
'A Practical Guide to the Law Relating to Food' by Ian Thomas

'A Practical Guide to Financial Services Claims' by Chris Hegarty
'The Law of Houses in Multiple Occupation: A Practical Guide to HMO Proceedings' by Julian Hunt
'A Practical Guide to Unlawful Eviction and Harassment' by Stephanie Lovegrove
'A Practical Guide to Solicitor and Client Costs' by Robin Dunne
'Occupiers, Highways and Defective Premises Claims: A Practical Guide Post-Jackson – 2nd Edition' by Andrew Mckie
'A Practical Guide to Financial Ombudsman Service Claims' by Adam Temple & Robert Scrivenor
'A Practical Guide to Advising Schools on Employment Law' by Jonathan Holden
'A Practical Guide to Running Housing Disrepair and Cavity Wall Claims: 2nd Edition' by Andrew Mckie & Ian Skeate
'A Practical Guide to Holiday Sickness Claims – 2nd Edition' by Andrew Mckie & Ian Skeate
'Arguments and Tactics for Personal Injury and Clinical Negligence Claims' by Dorian Williams
'A Practical Guide to QOCS and Fundamental Dishonesty' by James Bentley
'A Practical Guide to Drone Law' by Rufus Ballaster, Andrew Firman, Eleanor Clot
'A Practical Guide to Compliance for Personal Injury Firms Working With Claims Management Companies' by Paul Bennett
'A Practical Guide to the Landlord and Tenant Act 1954: Commercial Tenancies' by Richard Hayes & David Sawtell
'A Practical Guide to Dog Law for Owners and Others' by Andrea Pitt
'RTA Allegations of Fraud in a Post-Jackson Era: The Handbook – 2nd Edition' by Andrew Mckie
'RTA Personal Injury Claims: A Practical Guide Post-Jackson' by Andrew Mckie
'On Experts: CPR35 for Lawyers and Experts' by David Boyle
'An Introduction to Personal Injury Law' by David Boyle

‘A Practical Guide to Chronic Pain Claims’ by Pankaj Madan
‘A Practical Guide to Claims Arising from Fatal Accidents’ by James Patience
‘A Practical Guide to Subtle Brain Injury Claims’ by Pankaj Madan

www.ingramcontent.com/pod-product-compliance
Ingram Content Group UK Ltd.
Pitfield, Milton Keynes, MK11 3LW, UK
UKHW021239300926
15471UKWH00013B/761

9 781913 715380